Students'
Rights

by Kate Burns

LUCENT BOOKS

An imprint of Thomson Gale, a part of The Thomson Corporation

THOMSON

GALE

Detroit • New York • San Francisco • San Diego • New Haven, Conn. • Waterville, Maine • London • Munich

© 2007 Thomson Gale, a part of The Thomson Corporation.

Thomson and Star Logo are trademarks and Gale and Lucent Books are registered trademarks used herein under license.

For more information, contact
Lucent Books
27500 Drake Rd.
Farmington Hills, MI 48331-3535
Or you can visit our Internet site at http://www.gale.com

LIBRARY OF CONGRESS CATALOGING-IN-PUBLICATION DATA

Burns, Kate.
 Students' rights / by Kate Burns.
    p. cm.— (Hot topics)
 Includes bibliographical references and index.
 ISBN 1-59018-860-8 (hard cover : alk. paper)
 1. Right to education—United States. 2. Students—Civil rights—United States.
 I. Title. II. Series: Hot topics
 LC213.2.B87 2006
 379.2'6—dc22

                                                                2005033348

Printed in the United States of America

CONTENTS

FOREWORD

Young people today are bombarded with information. Aside from traditional sources such as newspapers, television, and the radio, they are inundated with a nearly continuous stream of data from electronic media. They send and receive e-mails and instant messages, read and write online "blogs," participate in chat rooms and forums, and surf the Web for hours. This trend is likely to continue. As Patricia Senn Breivik, the dean of university libraries at Wayne State University in Detroit, states, "Information overload will only increase in the future. By 2020, for example, the available body of information is expected to double every 73 days! How will these students find the information they need in this coming tidal wave of information?"

Ironically, this overabundance of information can actually impede efforts to understand complex issues. Whether the topic is abortion, the death penalty, gay rights, or obesity, the deluge of fact and opinion that floods the print and electronic media is overwhelming. The news media report the results of polls and studies that contradict one another. Cable news shows, talk radio programs, and newspaper editorials promote narrow viewpoints and omit facts that challenge their own political biases. The World Wide Web is an electronic minefield where legitimate scholars compete with the postings of ordinary citizens who may or may not be well-informed or capable of reasoned argument. At times, strongly worded testimonials and opinion pieces both in print and electronic media are presented as factual accounts.

Conflicting quotes and statistics can confuse even the most diligent researchers. A good example of this is the question of whether or not the death penalty deters crime. For instance, one study found that murders decreased by nearly one-third when the death penalty was reinstated in New York in 1995. Death penalty supporters cite this finding to support their argument that the existence of the death penalty deters criminals from committing murder. However, another study found that states without the death penalty have murder rates below the national average. This study is cited by opponents of capital punishment, who reject the claim that the death penalty deters murder. Students need context and clear, informed discussion if they are to think critically and make informed decisions.

The Hot Topics series is designed to help young people wade through the glut of fact, opinion, and rhetoric so that they can think critically about controversial issues. Only by reading and thinking critically will they be able to formulate a viewpoint that is not simply the parroted views of others. Each volume of the series focuses on one of today's most pressing social issues and provides a balanced overview of the topic. Carefully crafted narrative, fully documented primary and secondary source quotes, informative sidebars, and study questions all provide excellent starting points for research and discussion. Full-color photographs and charts enhance all volumes in the series. With its many useful features, the Hot Topics series is a valuable resource for young people struggling to understand the pressing issues of the modern era.

INTRODUCTION

SPECIAL PRIVILEGES, SPECIAL LIMITATIONS

The idea that a person's civil or constitutional rights might need special protections or have special limitations in a school setting is based on four main developments in American history. First came the notion that every citizen deserves an education, rooted in the Revolutionary period when democratic ideals of civil rights and civil liberties were enshrined in the U.S. Constitution and the Bill of Rights. Second, the idea that students should have input into their own education developed from student-centered ideas about teaching that first became popular at the turn of the twentieth century. Third, by the beginning of World War II, Americans began to understand youth, most of whom were students, as a distinct minority group. Finally, in the 1960s and 1970s, a time when other minority groups were demanding equality in American society, student activists gained significant victories that increased their rights in American education. All of these developments contribute to an ongoing debate about whether students should have limited or expanded civil liberties and rights, or the same constitutional protections as adult citizens in the United States.

Who Gets to Learn?

Historically, the first debate about students' rights arose over the question of whether everyone was entitled to a public education. As understood today, public education means schooling provided by the government and paid for by taxes; however, public education in America arose out of an early union between the church and the state. It was the Puritans of the Massachusetts Bay Colony during the seventeenth century who initiated the first state-sponsored schools whose curriculum combined religious and academic instruction for all boys and occasionally for girls. Outside of Puritan Massachusetts, though, religious diversity and class division made public education more challenging. It was the male children of wealthy landowners who consistently received an education, by tutors if no schools were available. Girls and women, poor children, indentured servants, and slaves often went without any formal schooling.

It was not until the Revolutionary period that a pioneering education agenda began to take shape. At this time, a new enthusiasm for civic duty to one's community outweighed the traditional emphasis on religious training that dominated schools for so many years. Influenced by the writing and ratification of the U.S. Constitution in 1789, American education began to take shape as a way to achieve national unity. Education was

UC Berkeley students, celebrating the fortieth anniversary of the Free Speech Movement in 2002, enjoy many freedoms once denied students at universities nationwide.

seen as an opportunity for economic and social mobility, and the development of youth into adults who could participate meaningfully in a democracy. Democratic values also pushed publicly funded schools to serve a wider range of youth, including children of the working classes.

THOSE WITH THE FEWEST RIGHTS?

Many pity youth as the most vulnerable group in society. But the reason they are so vulnerable is because society has intentionally made them vulnerable by affording them no civil rights.

Quoted in *One and Four*, "Rich Jahn Articulates a Defense of Youth Rights," October 5, 2005.

As industrial development took root in northern cities, it became clear that some sort of uniting institution was needed to build a common national identity among the diverse workers and immigrants who were flooding into the factories. At the turn of the nineteenth century, a humanitarian movement to provide free education to the children of the poor—including free schools for African American children—was thriving in the North. It was argued that children needed basic reading skills to work in the manufacturing trades, and that strong values and a love of learning helped to deter children from lives of crime or wickedness. More than ever before, the school was seen as the melting pot that could level economic differences, blend racial differences, and teach children what it meant to be American. As a result of that thinking, nineteenth-century court cases and legislation in the United States laid the foundation for the public support of schools from elementary to college levels. After the Civil War, the public school was at the forefront of the civil rights movement, continuing to find its way as an agency of and for the people.

The Student Takes Center Stage

In the early twentieth century, the concept became popular that education should adapt to the natural stages of childhood development rather than force children to conform to adult expectations of learning. This student-centered educational philosophy argued that children should be free to explore whatever interests caught their attention. Rather than focus on the teacher or the subject matter, student-centered schools allowed children to discover their own inspirations and develop their own values.

Even with this new attention on the student, up until the mid-twentieth century, few children attended school past the elementary level. Before World War II, children were expected to participate in family income earning, working either in the home, in factory jobs, or on the farm. Most assumed adult responsibilities by the age of twelve or thirteen. Their obligations left little time for school attendance.

HAVING TOO MANY RIGHTS IS HARMFUL

We've given high school students enough freedom to hurt their grades enough that they often fail and often drop out. For their own good, we should rethink those freedoms.

Sue Ontiveros, "Curtailing Freedom Could Help Kids Succeed in High School," *Chicago Sun Times*, June 25, 2005.

The circumstances of American childhood changed dramatically between 1945 and 1960. The rapid increase in the post–World War II population, called the baby boom, and postwar economic prosperity meant that more young people than ever before were free to attend school and associate with each other. Retailers and the entertainment industry recognized youth as a new market at leisure to spend money on clothes, amusement, popular culture, and the media. A youth movement began to develop and mature as the baby boomers came into their own during the 1960s and 1970s, still as students far more than as workers or family heads, demanding a space in American life for the expression of youth culture.

Along with this development, young people recognized their limited power and status in American society and began demanding more independence and power to make their own

Demonstrators rally in support of gay and lesbian students in New York City.

decisions. Student activism led to increased pressure for an expansion of student rights. In the 1980s and 1990s, students' rights issues came into the foreground of American society with court cases and legislation that further defined students' civil rights and civil liberties, and their appropriate limitations.

In the new millennium those liberties and limitations continue to evolve alongside new advances in technology that complicate classic students' rights issues. In particular, with the latest crop of young people nicknamed the "Wired Generation," the issues of access to information, freedom of expression, and privacy must be revisited in relation to students using the Internet and other electronic technology in school. It is likely that ever-developing innovations and social changes influencing education will ensure that students' rights remain a hot topic in American society for years to come.

The Right to Education Without Discrimination

Many would say that the most basic student right is the right to be a student; that is, to receive a free, equal, public education. Today, young people in most states have not only the *obligation* to go to school until they are sixteen years old, but the *right* to go to school, from kindergarten to high school, until they are twenty-one years old. The common belief is that education gives children the skills necessary to achieve the American Dream of increasing economic and social status, no matter where they start in life. Many Americans also link the "pursuit of happiness" expressed in the Declaration of Independence with the attainment of knowledge and the pure joy of learning. From the beginning, Americans have valued the freedom to improve their lot and seek personal fulfillment through education.

Yet history shows that Americans have disagreed over which people deserve the right to an education. They have also fought over what conditions and curricula must be provided to guarantee an equally good education for all students, regardless of sex, race, or ethnicity. Some of the most heated legal and cultural battles in American history have come from these disagreements.

Challenging "Separate but Equal" Education

Educational conflicts have played a major role in the modern civil rights movement. By the mid-twentieth century, many Americans agreed that all citizens, regardless of race, gender, or class, deserved the right to an education. However, laws or customs in most parts of the country still made sure that African American children attended schools that were segregated from those for white children. The 1896 Supreme Court decision in *Plessy v. Ferguson* was still in effect, declaring that "separate but equal" was the proper method of providing equal access to education for African Americans. Equality in education could be achieved, it was argued by many white Americans, without allowing racial minorities into all-white schools.

The actual schooling experience for many African American children, however, was far from equal to that of white children. For example, it was not uncommon in the deep southern states for black-only schools to be nothing more than ramshackle shanties. Secretary of Education Rod Paige describes his experience with segregation during his school years in Mississippi:

> The fact that [white students] had a gym was a big deal. They played basketball on the inside. They had a big gym with lights and stuff on the inside. We played bas-

A teacher conducts class for black students in a dilapidated Mississippi schoolhouse in 1939.

ketball on the outside with a clay court. We played up
until the time that you couldn't see the hoop any more.
. . . I wanted to take band, but there was no music.
I wanted to play football, but there was no football team
[until senior year]. . . . The concept of separate but equal
is not at all academic for me. It is very personal. And
even today . . . I don't know what I missed.[1]

The emerging civil rights movement of the 1950s gave voice
to the many African American parents and leaders who were
angered by the dishonesty they saw in the "separate but equal"
standard. They argued that *Plessy v. Ferguson* allowed whites to
maintain their prejudices and keep the best public education
resources for their own children. To them, segregated education
was simply a more sophisticated form of discrimination.

The controversy inspired one of the most famous civil rights
court cases in American history. On behalf of the National Association for the Advancement of Colored People (NAACP), a
young African American lawyer named Thurgood Marshall organized the case *Brown v. Board of Education of Topeka* against
several segregated school districts in the country. Marshall argued the case before the Supreme Court in December 1952; in
May 1954 the Court famously ruled, in Chief Justice Earl War-
ren's decision, that "separate educational facilities are inherently
unequal."[2] This decision overturned years of school segregation:
Suddenly the term "students' rights" applied to white *and* black
students alike.

Resistance to Desegregation

Brown v. Board of Education made segregation in American
schools illegal, but enforcing desegregation was another thing
entirely. The justices issued no specific deadlines to integrate
American schools, using a gradual approach that allowed opponents of the decision to organize massive resistance to school
desegregation. By 1956 more than one hundred members of
Congress signed a mandate called the Southern Manifesto and
promised to use "any lawful means" to topple the *Brown* decision.[3] A few scattered efforts to integrate schools in the late

1950s were met with intimidation, violence, and even bombings. Perhaps the most memorable instance of resistance was in 1957 when the white residents of Little Rock, Arkansas, lined both sides of the sidewalk leading to the front doors of Central High School to protest the enrollment of the school's first black students. They raised their fists and yelled insults at the handful of African American girls and boys walking toward the entrance. So tense was this situation that President Dwight D. Eisenhower deployed National Guard troops to Little Rock to maintain order and make sure the black students entered the school safely.

By 1964, ten years after the *Brown* decision, only 2 percent of African American students in the South were attending formerly white-only schools. Finally recognizing the need to enforce the law, Congress passed the Civil Rights Act of 1964. Among other measures, the act authorized the federal government to withhold funding from public schools that did not integrate their students. At last, the federal government could file school desegregation suits and pressure resistant districts to obey the law. In 1968 Marshall, now serving as the first African American Supreme Court justice, led the Court in requiring an immediate end to segregation, as he wrote, to destroy it "root and branch."[4]

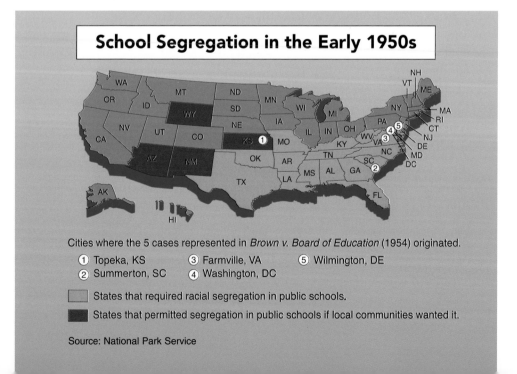

School Segregation in the Early 1950s

Cities where the 5 cases represented in *Brown v. Board of Education* (1954) originated.

① Topeka, KS   ③ Farmville, VA   ⑤ Wilmington, DE
② Summerton, SC   ④ Washington, DC

☐ States that required racial segregation in public schools.

■ States that permitted segregation in public schools if local communities wanted it.

Source: National Park Service

An African American girl endures taunting and intimidation as she bravely enters Central High School in Little Rock, Arkansas in 1957.

From the late 1960s until the late 1980s, rigorous federal and local programs helped to achieve more racial integration than ever before. Many school districts began a controversial program known as busing, transporting students outside of their neighborhoods to attend schools that previously had no racial mixing. As a result, racial diversity in the schools improved even in the South, where the number of African American students attending black-only schools fell from 80 percent to 55 percent between 1968 and 1988. Moreover, the predominantly black schools in southern states were provided with facilities and resources equal to those of predominantly white schools by 1990, and more African American teachers received salaries equal to those of white teachers.

The Right to Equality in Education for All Racial and Ethnic Minorities

As immigration changed the demographic landscape of the United States between the 1970s and the 1990s, the rights of other ethnic

Is Racial Discrimination in School Still a Problem?

A 2000 study titled *Facing the Consequences: An Examination of Racial Discrimination in U.S. Public Schools*, conducted by the Applied Research Center (ARC), reports compelling evidence that public schools consistently fail to provide the same quality of education for students of color as for white students. Their findings include:

- African American, Latino, and Native American students are suspended or expelled in numbers vastly disproportionate to those of their white peers. This was true in every school district surveyed. Furthermore, zero tolerance policies exacerbate this trend.

- Students of color are much more likely to drop out or be pushed out of school and less likely to graduate than white students. For example, in San Francisco, both Latino and African American students represented a percentage of dropouts in excess of their percentage of the population.

- Students of color have less access to advanced classes and gifted programs. The report shows that in all twelve school districts studied, students of color did not have fair access to Advanced Placement and gifted classes, which are essential to admission to many colleges.

- Most school districts do not require anti-racist or multi-cultural training for teachers and administrators. None of the twelve school districts had teaching staffs as diverse as their student population.

Terry Keleher, "National Study Uncovers Public School Racial Discrimination," Applied Research Center, March 1, 2000. www.arc.org/erase/FTCpress.html.

and racial minorities to a free public education also became an issue. The rising Latino and Asian American populations in many states revealed the shortcomings of desegregation discussions that focus exclusively on African American and white racial mixing. Many racial and ethnic minorities share a history of being excluded from public education. In California, for example, "Mongolians and Indians" along with "Negroes" were prohibited from attending school with white children in 1863. The strong suspicion and hatred of Chinese immigrants by Anglo-Americans in the nineteenth century was especially fierce in western territories such as California. In 1885 officials in San Francisco built a separate Oriental School, requiring Chinese, Japanese, and Korean children to stay away from white students. Some individual Asian Americans in smaller towns successfully resisted segregation, yet the courts did not end legal segregation in California until 1947.

In the same vein, many people assume that the plaintiffs in *Brown* were the first minorities to collectively challenge segregation in American education. However, that is far from the truth. As early as 1930, Mexican Americans were standing up to efforts in California and Texas to create separate schools for their children. For example, in Lemon Grove, California, school board officials claimed that Mexican American children, who often needed extra help acquiring English-language fluency, were slowing down the education of white students. The community made plans to build a school just for Mexican Americans, but their progress was interrupted when Mexican Americans in the border town filed suit against the school board for discriminating against Mexican American children. In 1931 they won their court case, *Alvarez v. Board of Trustees of the Lemon Grove School District*, and successfully prevented segregated education more than two decades before the landmark *Brown* decision.

Education for Illegal Immigrants

Closely related to the issue of educational access for Americans who are racial minorities is the issue of educational access for immigrants who are not American citizens. Like racial minorities, over the course of American history various immigrant groups, including Irish, Jewish, and southern European immigrants, were not welcomed into some public schools. Today, citizenship status is still a controversial issue in determining who has a right to be a student in the public school system.

The most heated controversy over the right to attend public schools today revolves around immigrants who have entered the United States illegally. Immigrant rights advocates argue that illegal immigrants are most often escaping extreme poverty or oppression in their home countries. They believe that a prosperous nation like America should help these individuals and the children they bring with them to thrive and become contributing citizens. All people should have the opportunity to improve their lives, and therefore improve the stability of the "nation of immigrants," as the United States has been called. Education, they argue, is the surest way to improve the economic prospects of potential citizens and undocumented workers.

However, other Americans object to the use of tax dollars to provide special services to immigrant students when their families do not pay income or property taxes. Organizations such as Americans for Legal Immigration (ALI) and the Federation for American Immigration Reform (FAIR) fight against providing any public education to illegal immigrants in the United States. Such organizations also object to providing public education to children born in the United States to illegal immigrants. "Every year, thousands of women enter the United States illegally to give birth," states FAIR, "knowing that their child will thus have U.S. citizenship. Their children immediately qualify for a slew of federal, state, and local benefit programs [including free public education]. . . . By not addressing this abuse, the funds that state and local governments must provide to [these] babies amounts to a virtual tax on U.S. citizens to subsidize illegal aliens."[5]

ILLEGAL IMMIGRANT CHILDREN DESERVE SPECIAL RIGHTS

[Legislation should] remove those federal barriers that keep immigrant children from reaching their highest potential. . . . If we want them to be productive, contributing members of society, we should encourage—not inhibit—their education. It is the right thing to do, and it's right for America.

Office of Congressman Chris Cannon, "Cannon Introduces the Student Adjustment Act, Designed to Help Children of Illegal Immigrants Gain Access to Higher-Ed," June 7, 2001. www.house.gov/cannon/press2001/Jun07.htm.

In response to these debates, Congress and the courts have delivered a range of decisions that convey an ambiguous legal stance in relation to immigrant educational rights. At times, the

Supreme Court has extended the right of public education to noncitizens who permanently live in the United States. In the 1982 case *Plyer v. Doe*, for example, the Court extended protection to noncitizens when it struck down a Texas law denying free public education to school-age children who were undocumented immigrants. In contrast, the federal government passed the Illegal Immigration Reform and Immigrant Responsibility Act of 1996, which barred illegal immigrants from receiving in-state tuition rates at public institutions of higher learning.

NO TUITION BREAKS FOR ILLEGAL IMMIGRANTS

In-state tuition for illegal immigrants is unfair across the board. Sometime soon, a legal California resident will lose his place at UC [the University of California] to an illegal alien. And that student's taxpaying parents will foot the bill.

Joe Guzzardi, "View from Lodi, CA: Illegal Immigrants Will Take Americans' College Places—at Taxpayer Expense," VDARE.com, February 1, 2002. www.vdare.com/guzzardi /cork.htm.

Individual states have also passed legislation defining the rights of illegal immigrants in relation to public education. In reaction to the federal law, voters in several states have approved laws allowing illegal immigrants to claim in-state tuition at state colleges and universities. In Kansas, for example, illegal immigrants can apply for in-state tuition if they have attended a Kansas high school for three years and are seeking legal immigrant status. In contrast, other states have passed legislation not only denying illegal immigrants in-state tuition breaks, but also denying them the right to go to public school at all. One prominent example is California's Proposition 187, which passed by a 59 percent margin of the vote in 1994. Proposition 187 declared that "only citizens of the United States and aliens lawfully admitted to the United States may receive the benefits of public social services,"[6] including health care and public education. The California proposition was killed by Governor Gray Davis in 1998, and the Kansas law is presently being challenged. Disputes over whether federal or state legislation has precedence have entered the courts, but they will not be definitively resolved until one of them reaches the Supreme Court.

Does Equality in Education Require Bilingual Education?

Most people agree that non-English-speaking immigrants who have entered the United States legally are entitled to attend public schools. However, the controversy over equality in relation to legal immigrants focuses on whether public schools are obliged to provide them with bilingual education or should instead require them to take classes only in English. Advocates of bilingual education do not belittle the importance of learning English; on the contrary, they believe it is much easier to learn English when students can use their native language as well. Laura Ferriero of the Mexican American Legal Defense and Educational Fund argues that "educational experts, Latino and otherwise, will tell you that bilingual education, when implemented properly, is the most effective way of teaching limited-English-proficient students."[7] In addition, advocates point out that immigrant students need to learn other core subjects, including math, social studies, science, and history, as well as English. In a bilingual setting, students can still keep up with these subjects while they also learn English. According to this viewpoint, denying students bilingual education is the same as denying them an education equal to that received by native speakers of English.

Many people disagree with this reasoning, including many immigrants themselves, and advocate instead the alternative to bilingual education often called English immersion or English-only education. Some opposed to bilingual education believe that it slows down the process of learning English. Others claim that officially allowing other languages to be taught and spoken in the public sector, including public schools, will diminish American unity. As Mauro E. Mujica, chairman of the lobby organization U.S. English, writes, "More than any form of government, democracies require interaction between the people and the governing bodies. . . . A shared method of communication

A young girl reads a book in Spanish in a dual-language first grade classroom in Kansas.

—a common language—is essential for this dynamic."[8] Mujica argues that bilingual education tends to discriminate against new immigrants by effectively channeling them into an ongoing state of second-class citizenship and dependency on government assistance. Without classes that enable rapid fluency in English, he believes, they are left vulnerable and isolated in America. From this point of view, bilingual education discriminates against immigrants rather than levels the educational experience.

Educational Equality for Girls and Women

Like racial minorities and immigrants, girls and women have sought equal access to education throughout American history. Historically, the education of girls and women has been secondary to that of boys and men. For centuries, women were thought to be intellectually inferior to men, and their education was considered unnecessary. Although girls were sometimes allowed to attend primary schools in colonial America, they were usually told to go home if all the classroom seats were taken by male students. After the American Revolution, this trend began to change somewhat. The former colonists had won independence from England to become citizens of a new nation, the United States of America. Their eagerness to build a strong union full of responsible citizens led to a higher appreciation of the role of women as mothers. Women were encouraged to learn to read and write in order to teach their sons about the Revolutionary ideas of liberty, freedom, and democracy in America.

Gradually, the prohibition against teaching girls and women lessened, and female students began to demand more educational opportunities. By the mid-1800s, women had begun to replace men as schoolteachers, largely because school districts

Students celebrate their graduation from Barnard College, an all-female college founded in 1889.

realized they could pay women lower wages than they paid men. Moreover, women gained more independence as the Industrial Revolution pushed them outside of the home to earn a living.

These changes inspired women to see themselves as worthy of the same rights that men took for granted. Along with fighting for the right to vote and own property, they fought for the right to attend all-male colleges and universities. Battles for access were waged one school at a time, and the doors to many institutions were opened only after years of protesting policies that barred women from higher education. Eventually, the rising legal and social status of women in society in general added to the pressure on all-male colleges and universities to become coeducational. Meanwhile, many colleges for women opened, delivering an education equal to that available at all-male schools. By 1900 an estimated one-third of resident college and university students were women. Publicly funded schools were often the first to grant access to women, while some private schools argued that since they were independent from the state, they had the right to exclude women.

Equal Access for Women

Even bigger changes were underway by the 1960s. The women's liberation movement compelled women to examine and challenge gender inequality in many areas of American life, including the home, the workplace, and the schools. The growing interest in equal access for women compelled Congress to pass Title IX of the Education Amendment Act in 1972. Title IX made it illegal for educational programs, public or private, to discriminate on the basis of a person's gender if the programs received federal funds. For school systems, this meant that a Title IX officer would monitor each school, help programs achieve equality, and handle complaints related to gender discrimination. If corrections were not made, federal funding was withdrawn. Some of the first programs to be affected were previously sex-segregated programs in health, vocational education, physical education, and higher levels of mathematics and science. Many people credit Title IX for the rapid advancement of women in higher education. By 1984, women obtained 49 percent of all undergraduate college degrees, and by 2003 more women than men—51 percent—were graduating from college.

Opening Military Academies to Women

In the 1970s women began to knock on the doors of the last bastion of all-male education: the military academy. Rather than rely on Title IX, several women turned to the Fourteenth Amendment to make a compelling argument for gender equality in education. When the Fourteenth Amendment was written it was not intended to protect women from discrimination, yet during the last quarter of the twentieth century, women's rights advocates successfully used the amendment to strike down laws that treated women differently than they treated men. The amendment states, "No State shall make or enforce any law which shall abridge the privileges or immunities of citizens of the United States; nor shall any State deprive any person of life, liberty, or property, without due process of law; nor deny to any person within its jurisdiction

A 1996 Supreme Court decision made it illegal for military academies like Virginia Military Institute (VMI) to deny admission to women.

the equal protection of the laws."[9] Advocates for gender equality argued that the spirit of nondiscrimination in the amendment should protect women as well as racial minorities.

During the mid-1990s, when increasing numbers of women took the issue to court, those who wanted to preserve male-only military academies refused to budge, claiming that allowing women into the schools would lower morale and undermine discipline. They argued that women do not and should not serve in combat positions, and therefore they should be educated differently than men. Many women's rights organizations countered that preventing women from obtaining the same military training and opportunities as men reinforces a second-place status for girls and women in American society.

In 1996 the debate went to the Supreme Court in the case of *United States v. Virginia.* Justices heard arguments about restricting admissions to the Virginia Military Institute (VMI) to men. During the controversy, the state of Virginia proposed a parallel program for women that would be equal to, but separate from, VMI. Citing the Fourteenth Amendment, the Court rejected the attempt and required VMI to admit both men and women.

What Kind of Teaching and Policies Provide an Equal Education?

Gaining access to educational opportunities has been an important goal for excluded groups in America. However, the struggle for education without discrimination does not stop with the issue of who is able to attend school. Once inside the school doors, minority groups and women alike have also demanded changes in traditional curricula and educational policies. An equal education, they argue, means that methods of instruction, course content, and cocurricular activities also enable them to learn and participate as fully as any other student.

Advocates of gender equity in schools base their concerns on evidence that girls and boys are treated differently by their peers, teachers, administrators, and school boards. For example, research conducted by the American Association of University Women (AAUW) indicates that girls face a pervasive bias against them in textbooks, teachers, and tests. The AAUW and other similar organizations argue that favoritism toward boys and lower expectations of girls end up shortchanging girls in significant ways. They believe that these additional barriers for girls in school tend to reduce their self-esteem, diminish their academic achievement, and lower their aspirations for higher education and successful careers. Without Title IX to enforce equality, they assert, it would be very difficult to motivate school boards and administrators to make the changes necessary for girls to receive an education equal to that of boys.

Title IX Changes in Academics and Athletics

Title IX has been used to make fields that have been traditionally male dominated more welcoming to girls and women. A case in point is math and science programs. Before Title IX, many teachers and administrators assumed that girls disliked math and science. It was common to steer girls away from math and science classes, and to discourage them from joining math and science clubs. After Title IX, many schools took steps to dispel the stereotype that girls could not excel in these fields. Now high school girls take the advanced math and science courses required to apply for college math and science majors at the same rate as boys. The Intercultural Development Research Association applauds the change, claiming in 2000 that "the enactment of Title IX 25 years ago removed many barriers to women and girls in the non-traditional fields of math and science, areas critical to their success in an increasingly technological world."[10] However, in a January 2005 speech during an academic conference, Harvard University president Lawrence H. Summers implied that Title IX and other such programs for girls and women may be futile solutions to the gender gap in science and math. He suggested that biological differences in male and female brains may explain why fewer women succeed in science and math careers, inherent differences that increasing girls' access will not erase.

Another area that has undergone adjustments is athletics, where girls' sports were long treated as less important than boys' sports. Although Title IX has received much media attention in relation to its impact on athletic programs, federal sanctions against schools that fail to follow the law have not been substan-

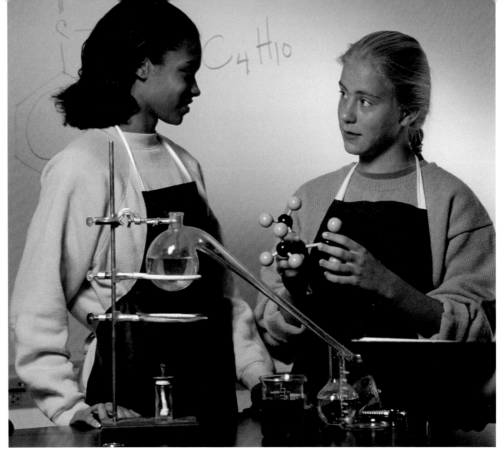

Two young women discuss a science project. Since the passage of Title IX in 1972 the gender gap in science and math has closed significantly.

tial, and the few sanctions that have been implemented remain highly controversial in the media and American public opinion.

Those who oppose Title IX often argue that the regulations are unnecessary and extreme. They point to increasing opportunities in society for girls and women that have already reduced the gender gap. The most vocal critics of Title IX tend to be male athletes and coaches who argue that requiring male and female athletic opportunities to be proportionately equal is excessive and actually discriminates against male students. T.J. Kerr, wrestling coach at California State University, Bakersfield, explains his position:

> School administrators believe that they must achieve proportionality. Many are unable, because of budget constraints, to add female sports programs, so these administrators drop male programs or "cap" sports by dropping

[male athletes]. Both of these approaches to achieving "gender equity" are wrong.[11]

Other critics of Title IX claim that boys and girls are naturally different and should be channeled into the activities that suit them best. Girls can excel in subjects like English, and boys are better in math and science, they state. Athletic programs should not be forced to provide equal opportunities for girls and women, according to this viewpoint, because they tend not to enjoy sports as much as boys and men do. This position has been highly controversial ever since the women's liberation movement and Title IX first began to challenge rigid gender roles and expectations.

American education has been marked by a long history of struggle over these two basic questions about equality in schooling: (1) Who deserves the right to have access to educational opportunities? and (2) What type of curricula, teaching methods, and policies constitute an equal education for all students? Early American prejudices excluded African Americans, other

Source: Jeff Parker, *Florida Today*/Cagle Cartoons.

Majority for Title IX Enforcement in Athletics

A 2000 *Wall Street Journal*/NBC News Poll asked two thousand adults these questions about Title IX:

> "Title Nine is a federal law that prohibits high schools and colleges that receive federal funds from discriminating on the basis of gender. Title Nine is most commonly invoked to ensure equal opportunities for girls and women in high school and college athletics. Do you approve or disapprove of Title Nine as it is described here?"

Yes, approve of Title IX: 79%

No, do not approve of Title IX: 14%

Do not know enough about it: 4%

Not sure: 3%

> "To comply with Title Nine, many schools and universities have had to cut back on resources for men's athletic programs and invest more in women's athletic programs to make the programs more equal. Do you approve or disapprove of cutting back on men's athletics to ensure equivalent athletic opportunities for women?"

Yes, approve of cuts: 76%

No, do not approve of cuts: 19%

Not sure: 5%

Quoted in Women's Sports Foundation, "Title IX—Possible Changes to Title IX Athletic Program Regulations: The Foundation Position," June 2002. www.womenssportsfoundation.org/cgi-bin/iowa/issues/rights/article. html?record=752.

racial and ethnic minorities, and women from full citizenship. Some of the people in charge of education declared that it was wasteful and even dangerous to educate those who were supposedly incapable of handling the rights and responsibilities of being a citizen of the United States. As each excluded group wrestled to prove their competence and therefore gain the rights of full citizenship, their opportunities in education began to open up as well.

STUDENTS' FREEDOM
OF SPEECH

What do the Pledge of Allegiance, hairstyles, political protests, campaign speeches, and racial slurs have in common? All of these topics have been important in debates about whether students have the same right to freedom of speech as other citizens do outside of an educational context. The right to "speak" actually implies the broader right of free expression. The First Amendment protects not only written or spoken words, but what the Supreme Court calls "expressive conduct," or actions that do not literally involve speaking or writing yet nonetheless send a message. Expressive conduct for students can include personal appearance—hair length, clothing, body piercings, and tattoos—as well as classroom essays, student assembly presentations, and online journals or blogs.

Outside the classroom, conflicts over freedom of speech often come down to different perspectives in relation to two cherished American values. One viewpoint insists on the importance of preserving individual civil liberties, including an individual's freedom of speech. The other viewpoint argues that protecting the interests of the community or society in general—that is, the safety and welfare of the people—must take precedence over the rights of any single individual. Many conflicts over free speech come about when someone claims that another person's speech is offensive, obscene, hateful, or likely to lead to violence. Legislation, courtroom decisions, and policies throughout American history have left a long record of the efforts to balance both values justly.

When freedom of speech becomes a concern in school, another consideration is added to the debate. A student's civil liberty is weighed not only against the good of the community, but also against the educational mission of the school. This additional element sometimes makes free speech conflicts in education even more complicated than those in society in general.

Must Students Recite the Pledge of Allegiance?

When educators talk about the purpose of public education, many bring up the importance of teaching young people how to be good citizens. Learning about American history and democratic values, it is argued, helps children understand the rights

Students recite the Pledge of Allegiance, a ritual that some feel should be banned from the classroom.

and responsibilities of citizenship they eventually will assume as adults. Certain practices associated with the idea have been the subject of debate over students' freedom of speech.

For example, one traditional expression of civic pride is the communal daily recitation of the Pledge of Allegiance in classrooms to encourage loyalty to and cultivate common values in the United States of America. The original pledge was written by Francis Bellamy in 1892 as a statement of patriotism; its well-known text reads, "I pledge allegiance to the Flag and the Republic for which it stands, one nation indivisible, with liberty and justice for all." By the 1920s reciting the pledge had become a ritual in many public schools.

In 1954 Congress voted to add the language "under God" to the original pledge in an effort to distinguish the United States from its Cold War enemy, the Soviet Union, a Communist, and in practice atheistic, government. President Eisenhower signed the Pledge of Allegiance bill from Congress on Flag Day, saying that now "millions of our schoolchildren will daily proclaim in every city and town . . . the dedication of our nation and our people to the Almighty."[12] To some Americans, the changed language of the pledge is an unconstitutional imposition of religion on the part of government.

A Major Free Speech Debate

The pledge has inspired a major debate related to freedom of speech for students on more than religious grounds. Some believe that requiring children to recite a pledge that they might not even understand is morally wrong. They argue that the pledge forces students to express a particular political viewpoint whether or not they agree with that viewpoint. According to opponents of the pledge, students in a democratic nation should have the freedom to develop their own political opinions and expressions of patriotism, just as adults do. Others point out that some religions, like the Jehovah's Witness faith, do not believe in swearing loyalty to any power less than God. Forcing members of the Jehovah's Witnesses to break their religious convictions and recite a pledge to the nation, they say, is a violation of the free speech and freedom of religion protected by the First Amendment.

Officially, the debate about whether or not to compel students to recite the pledge was resolved more than seventy years ago in the 1943 Supreme Court case *West Virginia Board of Education v. Barnette*. At that time schoolchildren were expected to raise their right hands in salute at the beginning of the day while they recited the Pledge of Allegiance. Children of the Jehovah's Witness faith faced widespread persecution when they refused to salute the flag. Some were expelled from school and threatened with being sent to reformatories for delinquent youth. When the suit protesting such treatment reached the Supreme Court, the practice was struck down as unconstitutional. Students had the right to opt out of saluting and saying the pledge if it went against their political or religious beliefs.

A STUDENT DESCRIBES THE CONSEQUENCES OF NOT SAYING THE PLEDGE

An unknown number of students are reprimanded every year for not saying the Pledge of Allegiance. They may receive detention, be sent to the principal's office, be suspended, or face other such punishment.

Ben Livingston, "Pledge Allegiance . . . or Else," *Oblivion*, Spring 2000. www.oblivion.net /oblivion/9/pledge.php3.

But *West Virginia Board of Education v. Barnette* did not end the conflict over the issue. Some schools chose not to abide by the decision and continued in various ways to punish or stigmatize students who refused to stand and recite the pledge. In his research for the First Amendment Center, attorney David L. Hudson Jr. reports, "In March 1998, a 13-year-old Jehovah's Witness in a Seattle middle school was forced to stand outside in the rain for 15 minutes for refusing to say the pledge. In April 1998, a 16-year-old student in San Diego was forced to serve detention for her failure to recite the pledge."[13] Hudson notes that a recent surge of patriotism after the September 11, 2001, terrorist attacks has fueled new efforts to require all students to recite the pledge in order to demonstrate their solidarity with

and allegiance to the United States. This rationale makes some Americans uneasy: Forcing juveniles to "prove" their loyalty through mandatory oaths strikes many as an erosion of First Amendment protections, particularly since no such loyalty test is required of the general public. Others counter that national loyalty must be instilled at an early age in order to ensure that all children will grow up to be good citizens.

Dress Codes and Free Expression

Another controversy over students' freedom of expression concerns school dress codes and mandatory uniforms. Do the clothing and appearance of students fall under the umbrella of the educational mission of schools or the freedom of expression of individual students? Compelling arguments have been made on both sides of the issue. There have been dress codes ever since schools began in the United States. Correspondingly, throughout the history of American education, students have rebelled against dress codes by making their own choices about their appearance.

Sometimes dress-code conflict is a matter of getting schools to adjust to current fashion trends, which come and go. Sometimes, however, dress-code conflict is a reflection of wider social rebellion or tests of authority. In the 1960s and 1970s, for example, the baby boomer youth culture encouraged boys and men to wear their hair long as an antiestablishment statement as well as a fashion trend. Since short hair had been the norm in previous decades, students and school codes clashed and the dispute ended up in court.

In numerous legal cases, the courts upheld the right of school administrators to regulate the length of male students' hair. For example, in the 1972 case *Karr v. Schmidt*, Fifth Circuit judge Lewis R. Morgan stated that "the right to style one's hair as one pleases in the public schools does not inherit the protection of the First Amendment."[14] More important than a student's right to hair length, he argued, is the school's intention to eliminate

In the 1960s and 70s, many young men wore their hair long as a political statement but the courts often upheld schools' attempts to regulate male hair length.

classroom distraction, prevent violence between long- and short-haired students, and eliminate health and safety hazards caused by long hairstyles. However, some judges wrote dissenting opinions indicating that such a regulation infringed on the rightful liberty of students because hair length can be a symbol of group affinity and nonconformity—in other words, it can be a personal and political statement.

Debates about student clothing are often related to conflicts over different moral values. For example, in 2002, administrators at a Florida high school required different standards of dress for male and female students because they believed men and women should be taught different sets of moral standards. The school's policy for the graduation ceremony required boys to wear nice pants and girls to wear dresses. Two students, Alicia Traurig and Amber Smith, wanted to wear slacks rather than dresses. They hired an attorney to represent their position opposing different dress-code standards based on gender. The attorney wrote a letter arguing that the high school's policy unfairly discriminates against female students in violation of the

Does Clothing Count as Self-Expression?

Kate Hess, a student at Freedom High School in Bethlehem, Pennsylvania, objects to school dress-code restrictions:

Many times, clothing is what students use to express themselves because they don't know how to phrase what they are trying to say. Sometimes, we feel so passionately about things that the words just don't seem to come out right, so we rely on others to help us.

Knowing this is the last form of freedom some of us have, the administrations and governments seek to force us to see their point of view on lots of things. Therefore controlling us, destroying our individuality, and denying us our first amendment right in one go.

Quoted in Youth Free Expression Network, "Should Students Be Required to Wear School Uniforms?" www.yfen.org/pages/message/message_board.htm.

Body piercing and tattooing have become increasingly popular forms of self-expression among young people.

students' constitutional right to privacy, liberty, and First Amendment protections. In this instance, the school decided to do away with the policy rather than face further resistance. Other schools in the district, however, have kept their separate requirements for girls' and boys' clothing. No cases have gone to court to set a legal precedent on the matter.

Similar struggles over what constitutes "proper" school appearance and clothing have erupted in recent years as tattooing and body piercing have become popular as fashion and self-expression for teens. In most states it is illegal to give someone under the age of eighteen a tattoo without parental consent. Nevertheless, some teens do obtain parental consent, and others get tattoos illicitly. In an effort to discourage minors from getting tattoos, South Carolina has instituted a ban on displaying tattoos in school. In support of the ban, South Carolina state senator Jakie Knotts made the statement, "If God wanted you to have a tattoo, you would have been born with one. . . . I just don't believe in marking up the body that the good Lord gave you."[15] On the other side of the issue, writer Shannon Larratt argues that body modifications such as tattoos and piercings are a biological instinct for some people. Self-decoration can be enormously positive to the self-definition and self-acceptance of teens. According to Larratt, denying teens this outlet for expression can cause depression and antisocial behavior. Schools have the moral obligation to empower teenagers, she says, not to demean them by removing their sense of autonomy over their bodies.

Other educators counter that regulating things like student appearance and dress are matters of school safety rather than moral differences. Some administrators have argued, for example, that students who get into an altercation or are active during recess are at a greater risk of injury if they have jewelry attached through piercings. Those who disagree point out that non-piercing-related jewelry can be just as risky, but earrings, necklaces, and bracelets are rarely banned in schools. They also say that requirements that force students to take out piercings at the start of the day and then put them back in after school ends are actually more dangerous for the student. The student is forced to go through school with an open piercing that is more likely to become infected. So far, no court cases have resulted from this issue.

Freedom to Protest

Resistance to dress codes sometimes goes hand in hand with other forms of student protest. Many people think of the defiance of the youth-led countercultural movement during the 1960s when they relate expression through appearance with political protest. Yet politically conscious college students began insisting on their right to free speech as early as 1905 when the muckraking novelist Upton Sinclair founded the Intercollegiate Socialist Society (ISS). Sinclair and other ISS members raised political questions and debates about socialism that educational institutions were reluctant to address in the classroom for fear of governmental disapproval and social scorn. In later years, student activists spoke out against the oppression of poor immigrants, women, and racial minorities, and led a substantial protest against the impending war in the late 1930s. However, the atmosphere of political repression during the 1950s, when Sen. Joseph McCarthy led investigations of those suspected of "Un-American activities," curtailed most student free speech activism until the early 1960s. At that time, several cultural elements came together to produce the most dramatic student movement for free speech in the history of the United States. The burgeoning baby boom generation led a countercultural movement that celebrated freedom of expression by the largest youth population in the United States up to that date.

Student free expression has been met with mixed reactions. Those who defend student speech argue that young people should have the same rights as adults. They warn against suppressing the

Source: Larry Wright, *The Detroit News*/Cagle Cartoons.

views of a substantial group of people who contribute important perspectives on a variety of issues. For these advocates, free speech is an essential tool for teaching young people to participate in a democratic nation. On the other hand, those who favor limiting student speech tend to believe that young people are not yet able to meet the responsibilities of full citizenship. To them, absolute free speech can disrupt the cooperative environment necessary to provide young people a quality education.

The argument was important for a well-known Supreme Court case that considered freedom of expression in public schools. *Tinker v. Des Moines Independent Community School District* was a 1969 case involving students who wore armbands to school in protest of the Vietnam War. The students' right to conduct this silent method of protest was upheld by the courts, largely because it was found that their expression did not disrupt class work or otherwise impede the educational operation of the school.

Protecting the Educational Mission of Schools

While some educators agree with the *Tinker* standard of free speech for students, other teachers and administrators believe that unlimited free expression can undermine their ability to maintain a high quality of learning in their schools. In some instances, the Supreme Court agreed that student expression should be curtailed when it disrupts the educational process of the school.

In *Bethel School District No. 403 v. Fraser* (1986), a high school student presented a student campaign speech laced with clever sexual connotations to his peers. The reaction from the student body was predictably boisterous. The student who gave the speech was suspended from school, but he claimed his First Amendment rights had been violated. The Supreme Court, however, disagreed, observing that the speech created a disruptive environment and that it sanctioned lewd and indecent conduct. In a landmark 1987 case associated with the student press, *Hazelwood School District v. Kuhlmeier*, the Supreme Court found that student expression can be regulated if it is without educational value or merit, as determined by school officials. Some students have publicly questioned whether such limits on students' speech limit young people in a way that is inconsistent with American educational values. For example, after her own battle with school officials over freedom of expression in 2000, high school student Jennifer Boccia asked:

> Do they honestly think that by teaching kids to sit down, shut up, and not question the whims of authority any time there is a "crisis," that in 30 years we will still have a democratic society? People have fought and suffered and died for these rights, and I'm supposed to give them up because a petty school official threatens to suspend me? No thanks.[16]

Violent Speech

Limitations to students' freedom of speech are less controversial when the speaker threatens the safety of other people. What if a student's words depict graphic violence against others in the school environment? One such case involved a Pennsylvania middle school student with the initials "J.S.," who created a Web site titled "Teacher Sux" in 1998. On his homepage, he made derogatory comments about the principal and a teacher. In itself, this was probably no different from millions of other student complaints in all times and places. What got J.S. into trouble was his drawing of the teacher's severed head dripping with blood. He also asked visitors to the site to send him a ten-dollar contribution to hire a hit man. The school district argued that the site was a clear threat to the teacher and promoted harm to the health, safety, and welfare of the school community. In 2000 the case *J.S. v. Bethlehem Area School District* went to the U.S. Supreme Court.

Although the Court agreed that off-campus student speech was generally protected by previous rulings, it cited the case of *Bethel School District No. 403 v. Fraser* in deciding that "the schools, as instruments of the state, may determine that the essential lessons of civil, mature conduct cannot be conveyed in a school that tolerates lewd, indecent, or offensive speech and conduct."[17] Such speech is not protected by the First Amendment. The Court upheld the school's action to suspend J.S.

A Michigan Student Defends His Right to Free Speech

Excerpts from an American Civil Liberties Union press release, May 10, 2004:

Timothy Gies, a senior at Bay City Central High School, was suspended on April 7 for five days for wearing a t-shirt with the anarchy symbol. School administrators had previously prohibited him from wearing peace signs, upside-down American flags and a sweatshirt with an anti-war quote from Albert Einstein, either by suspending him or by insisting that he take off the t-shirt or sweatshirt he was wearing. . . .

When Gies contended that he had a First Amendment right to express himself, one administrator informed him that the Constitution does not apply to Bay City students. Another mockingly told him to report the incident to the ACLU. He did exactly that. . . .

[In May 2004] Timothy received a letter stating that because the shirt was neither threatening nor disruptive, the discipline would be set aside. In addition to reversing Gies' suspension, the administration has agreed to allow students to wear other political symbols on their clothing.

"I believe that in order to adequately prepare students for the future, they must be exposed to a diverse, cross-section of people and ideas," Gies said. "The fight for our right to free expression was a hard one and even though I'm graduating in June, I'll rest easy knowing that next year's class will be able to share ideas without being punished."

American Civil Liberties Union, "Michigan School Reverses Student's Suspension for Wearing 'Anarchy' T-Shirt," May 10, 2004. www.aclu.org/studentsrights/expression/12846prs20040510.html.

Many parents, teachers, and school administrators agree with the Pennsylvania decision, especially after the infamous Columbine High School massacre in 1999, when Eric Harris and Dylan Klebold opened fire on their schoolmates in Littleton, Colorado, killing twelve students and a teacher. They argue that if a student's speech crosses the line and threatens actual physical harm—such as Harris did on his Internet "hit list" before the incident at Columbine—then schools must take the threat seriously, and limitations on free expression are justified.

Legal analysts Mike Hiestand and Mark Goodman disagree with the *J.S. v. Bethlehem School District* decision, arguing that off-campus expression should not be limited: "For many high school students today, the opportunity to express themselves in a school-sponsored medium without administrative censorship

Columbine High School students grieve at a memorial. The courts have ruled that the First Amendment does not protect threatening off-campus speech such as the Columbine killers' Internet "hit list."

has been all but eliminated. The Internet has created a meaningful alternative."[18] To critics like Hiestand and Goodman, extending schools' jurisdiction over student speech to the Internet is a violation of the civil liberties of young people. This aspect of the debate over student free speech continues to grow more complex as innovative technologies such as instant messaging and text messaging introduce new venues for expression.

Campus Speech Codes

The issue of regulating offensive student speech involves more than threats of physical violence, of course. An even more contentious controversy has arisen on college campuses over whether to regulate hostile or discriminatory speech—generally called hate speech—especially when it is directed toward a person's race, ethnicity, gender, religion, or sexual orientation. Regulating violent speech is one thing, but what about regulating hate speech?

CENSORSHIP HARMS EDUCATION

We are disturbed by the trend among public schools to crack down on students' rights to free expression. Unless the speech causes a major disruption of the school, schools cannot ban it. The solution to bad speech is more speech, not censorship.

Kary Moss, executive director of the ACLU of Michigan, quoted in American Civil Liberties Union, "Michigan School Reverses Student's Suspension for Wearing 'Anarchy' T-Shirt," May 10, 2004. www.aclu.org/studentsrights/expression/12846prs20040510.html.

In an effort to create a welcoming climate to all students, some college campuses have instituted speech codes that restrict expressions of hate speech. Some opponents of such hate speech policies argue that antiharassment restrictions curtail students' free speech. Others hold that all students, regardless of their identities or backgrounds, should have the right to attend school free of harassment and discrimination, and therefore any attack based on their identity should be punished. Federal appeals court cases have agreed, requiring schools to take steps to eliminate harassment once they become aware of it. For example, in the 2003 case *Flores v. Morgan Hill Unified School District*, the court affirmed that schools can be held liable when they deliberately ignore harassment of gay students.

However, the boundaries defining hate speech are not yet settled. In 2001, for example, a federal district court overturned a Pennsylvania school district's policy because it prohibited speech that did little more than cause hurt feelings. Organizations like the American Civil Liberties Union argue that school administrations can find an appropriate balance between preventing harassment and respecting students' First Amendment rights.

The debate about whether limits on free expression can be justified extends far beyond high school and college campuses. As the above examples show, censorship of speech and other student expression occurs for a number of reasons, from the trivial to the personal to the political. Political speech may get the most attention, but court decisions in the wake of *Hazelwood* show that speech does not have to be overtly inflammatory in order to be restricted. Regardless of the reasons, the infringement of campus free expression—and free speech outside the educational system—continues to be a controversial issue.

THE RIGHTS OF THE STUDENT PRESS

Most students assume that freedom of the press was clearly established when Americans ratified the First Amendment in 1791. From the beginning, citizens of the United States supported rigorous and fearless journalism as the birthright of their new nation. Like many of the Founding Fathers, Thomas Jefferson argued that a democracy could thrive only if its citizens were educated and informed. He believed that a free press was an essential avenue of education and information. In 1787 he wrote: "The basis of our government being the opinion of the people, the very first object should be to keep that right; and were it left to me to decide whether we should have a government without newspapers, or newspapers without government, I should not hesitate a moment to prefer the latter."[19]

Yet the First Amendment's ability to protect freedom of the press was not truly tested until the twentieth century, when landmark decisions in the Supreme Court clearly established the constitutional understanding that media freedom is vital to maintaining a democratic and accountable government. In 1964 the Court confirmed in the case of *New York Times Co. v. Sullivan* a "profound national commitment to the principle that debate on public issues should be uninhibited, robust, and wide-open, and that it may well include vehement, caustic and sometimes unpleasantly sharp attacks on government and public officials."[20]

Nevertheless, Americans have disagreed about whether student journalists should have the same rights as adult journalists. Since student media is produced in an educational setting, some fear that absolutely uncensored publications could interrupt the educational purposes of schools. Others question the wisdom of granting unlimited forums to youthful reporters who may not fully understand the risks, responsibilities, and possible consequences of what they publish. Those who oppose censorship of the student press argue that an essential purpose of American education is to provide experiences for students to learn about the rights and responsibilities of citizenship, and that those experiences should mirror real-world journalism. Advocates tend to believe that students need and deserve avenues for editorial and creative as well as journalistic training just as much as the general public does.

School Sponsorship Leads to School Censorship

Some of the earliest student newspapers included the *Student Gazette* of Penn Charter School in Philadelphia (begun in 1777), and the *Literary Journal* of Boston Latin School (begun in 1829). These newspapers, however, were run by groups of students working on their own rather than by the schools themselves. This model changed when journalism became an optional class in high schools in 1912, and soon journalism classes were expected to produce a school newspaper as part of the learning experience.

This development changed the nature of the student press. Historian Nicholas D. Kristof observes:

> With school support, student newspapers became more professional—in the sense that the writing was better and that they looked more like commercial newspapers. But they also became more like house public relations newsletters, with the expectation that they would propagandize for the school and cover only "good news." The result was a tension between increased professionalism, which implied aggressive, skeptical reporting, and the tendency of administrators to see the school newspaper as a public relations tool.[21]

When student journalists sought to report content beyond school social and athletic activities, and to increase their critical stance in relation to school policies and local or national politics, they began to encounter resistance by teachers or school administrators. In some instances, school officials refused permission to print what they saw as offensive or controversial material. Until the mid-twentieth century, it was generally accepted that administrators, teachers, and advisers had the authority to review student publications and repress sensitive or controversial material.

Conflicts over censorship in student newspapers increased as a result of the political unrest among students during the 1960s. In response to censorship of their official school newspapers, students sometimes started "underground" papers that

These students filed a lawsuit to stop their high school principal from censoring articles on homosexuality in the student newspaper.

they produced off the school campus. The independence allowed them to report content and express views that school officials condemned. Students in Madison, Wisconsin, for example, went off their high school campus to produce the underground newspaper *Links* in the late 1960s. Their mission statement expressed their desire for more freedom of speech:

> We started [*Links*] because the regular press just doesn't meet the needs of young people throughout the state. The issues which directly affect us are ignored by established press and "official" high school papers. . . . *Links* is an attempt . . . to build our own means of communication, our own media, controlled by us, and through which our ideas, beliefs, and experiences can be freely and fully expressed.[22]

STOP CENSORSHIP OF STUDENT NEWSPAPERS

Censorship is the fundamental cause of the triviality, innocuousness and uniformity that characterize[s] high school press. Where a free, vigorous student press does exist, there is a healthy ferment of ideas and opinions with no indication of disruption or negative side effects on the educational experience of the school.

Scholastic.com, "The *Hazelwood* Decision and the Student Press: A Complete Guide to the Supreme Court Decision," http://teacher.scholastic.com/researchtools/articlearchives /civics/usgovt/judic/hazs tupr.htm.

The tension between administrators seeking more control over school newspapers and student reporters seeking greater freedom continues to fuel the debate about the appropriate degree of freedom of the press in education. Struggles over the issue have resulted in landmark Supreme Court cases that define the legal boundaries of student press freedom. Legal cases have defined the rights of the student press at both the high school and college or university levels. Moreover, now that the Internet has become a popular forum for expression in America, the courts are beginning to address freedom of student online publications.

Tinker Protects the High School Student Press

Before the 1980s, public high school administrators were limited by the Supreme Court decision in *Tinker v. Des Moines Independent Community School District* when they wanted to suppress the free speech of students. The case involved several high school students in Des Moines, Iowa, who wore black armbands to their schools in protest of the U.S. government's involvement in the Vietnam War. When the principals of the schools suspended them for their silent protest, the students filed suit, arguing that their First Amendment right to free expression was violated. On February 24, 1969, the Supreme Court ruled in favor of the teenagers on the grounds that students do not "shed their constitutional rights to freedom of speech or expression at the schoolhouse gate."[23]

Although the case involved a particular form of expression —displaying a symbol of protest—that was quite different from publishing articles, it greatly affected the world of student journalism. For almost twenty years after the decision, *Tinker* set the standard for recognizing students' right to free expression, including the right to publish their observations and opinions in student newspapers. It wasn't until 1988 that the rights of high school students were definitively set apart from those of college students in the landmark Supreme Court case *Hazelwood School District v. Kuhlmeier.*

Hazelwood Limits Freedom of the High School Student Press

Hazelwood is the precedent-setting case that limits the rights of free speech for students in public high schools in the United States today. The original lawsuit was initiated in 1983 by three students who had graduated from Hazelwood East High School just outside of Saint Louis, Missouri. The students had worked on the year's final issue of the school newspaper, the *Spectrum*, in which they featured a special "teen issue" section including an article describing several students' experiences with pregnancy and another article discussing the impact of divorce on students at Hazelwood.

Hazelwood principal Robert Reynolds holds a copy of the school newspaper, the Spectrum. *In 1988 the Supreme Court upheld Reynolds's decision to censor articles about pregnancy and divorce.*

The *Spectrum* was written and edited by a journalism class as part of the school's curriculum. The newspaper's policy at the time was for the journalism teacher to submit the page proofs to the school's principal for approval before publication. When Hazelwood principal Robert Reynolds read the pregnancy and divorce stories in the page proofs of this particular issue, he decided to delete the two pages of the *Spectrum* containing the controversial articles. He objected to the pregnancy story because he feared the pregnant students, although not named in the article, could be identified from other details in the text. In addition to his desire to protect their privacy, he also felt that the article's discussion of sexual activity and birth control was unsuitable for younger students who may read the *Spectrum*. He believed the article about divorce should be censored because it contained sharp criticism from a student about her father. Reynolds believed the student's parents should have been given an opportunity to respond to her remarks or to consent to their publication. Reynolds's superiors agreed with his decision.

The three student members of the *Spectrum* staff filed suit against the Hazelwood School District and school officials, and the case was appealed all the way to the Supreme Court, much like the *Tinker* case. *Hazelwood* was decided on January 13, 1988. In striking contrast to decisions handed down since *Tinker*, the Supreme Court ruled in favor of the principal who censored the controversial stories in the *Spectrum*. *Hazelwood* now allows school officials to edit and censor school publications that are produced as part of a class. As long as the school has no additional "policy or practice" that expands the freedom of its student press, administrators can make the final decisions about what will be published and what will not appear in a school newspaper. However, limiting free expression is allowed only if the school officials demonstrate a reasonable educational explanation for doing so. In other words, principals and teachers must not prevent an article from being published merely because they disagree with a student's viewpoint.

Prior Restraint: Censorship or Protection?

Administrators have used methods other than outright censorship to gain more control over school newspapers. In some instances, principals have seized all copies of a newspaper after it has been published in order to prevent its distribution. One of the first post-*Hazelwood* cases brought this issue to the attention of the American public. The incident took place after students published an article in an Ohio high school newspaper alleging that the Wooster City School Board violated its own underage drinking policy by giving preferential treatment to athletes caught drinking. Wooster High School's principal seized all copies of the newspaper after it was printed. His concern was that the article quoted a student athlete who admitted to drinking and that the article was potentially defamatory to the student.

Members of the paper filed suit, claiming the confiscation of the papers amounted to "prior restraint" of speech, or preventative censorship, in violation of the First Amendment. The district court determined that the policy on student media established by the Wooster City School Board gave it the right to use prior restraint and therefore prevent distribution of the newspaper. Before the case went to court, the school board had classified the student media as "publications which are not protected by the right of free expression because they violate the rights of others, such as material that defames any specific person(s)."[24] Since the Wooster High School principal was worried about the football player's reputation, the court supported his confiscation of the newspapers.

Public and Nonpublic Forums

The 2003 *Draudt v. Wooster City School District Board of Education* decision also further clarified the distinction between "public" and "nonpublic" forum publications in relation to school environments. Legally, a public forum is defined as a place that is generally used by the public for speech-related purposes. In the school setting, a newspaper is a public forum when the administration has given student editors the authority to make

Three Supreme Court Justices Disagree with the *Hazelwood* Decision

Excerpts from the dissenting opinion from Justices Brennan, Marshall, and Blackmun in *Hazelwood v. Kuhlmeier:*

When the young men and women of Hazelwood East High School registered for Journalism II, they expected a civics lesson. *Spectrum*, the newspaper they were to publish, "was not just a class exercise in which students learned to prepare papers and hone writing skills, it was a . . . forum established to give students an opportunity to express their views while gaining an appreciation of their rights and responsibilities under the First Amendment to the United States Constitution. . . ."

In my view the principal . . . violated the First Amendment's prohibitions against censorship of any student expression that neither disrupts classwork nor invades the rights of others, and against any censorship that is not narrowly tailored to serve its purpose.

William J. Brennan Jr., dissenting opinion, *Hazelwood School District v. Kuhlmeier* 484 U.S. 260 (1988).

High school students protest the seizure of their student-produced newspaper by school officials, who intended to reprint and distribute a censored version.

their own content decisions. The government is not allowed to restrict the content of speech in a public forum unless it can show that a compelling governmental interest is at stake; for example, secret military strategies can be censored if revealing them could threaten national security.

Before *Draudt*, the Supreme Court's *Hazelwood* decision declared that high school newspapers that are produced in journalism classes are nonpublic forum publications because editorial decisions are ultimately made by the journalism teacher or the school principal. However, it was in the *Draudt* case that the court developed criteria distinguishing such publications from school newspapers produced in a club or cocurricular setting, or a "limited public forum" that has *some* history of student-based editorial decisions. Publications produced in a limited public forum have more First Amendment protections than nonpublic forum newspapers. The advocacy organization First Amendment Schools (FAS) explains:

> The government can limit access to certain types of speakers in a limited public forum, or limit the use of such facilities for certain subjects. Despite these more proscriptive guidelines, however, a governmental institution may still not restrict expression at a limited forum unless that restriction serves a "compelling interest."[25]

Although the school newspaper in *Draudt v. Wooster* was found to be a limited public forum, the students lost their legal case for other reasons. Yet *Draudt* is important because it determined that high school publications classified as public or limited public forums are protected by the much higher *Tinker*-based standard rather than the *Hazelwood* standard. Thus, in order to

U.S. Teens "Reject" Key Freedoms

Excerpts from a *BBC News* online article:

A significant number of US high-school students regard their constitutional right to freedom of speech as excessive, according to a new survey.

Over a third of the 100,000 students questioned felt the First Amendment went "too far" in guaranteeing freedom of speech, press, worship and assembly.

Only half felt newspapers should be allowed to publish stories that did not have the government's approval. . . .

The president of the John S. and James L. Knight Foundation, which conducted the research, said, "Ignorance about the basics of this free society is a danger to this nation's future."

The survey concluded that better teaching and a bigger emphasis on student journalism could raise awareness of the First Amendment in American classrooms.

BBC News, "US Teens 'Reject' Key Freedoms," February 1, 2005. http://news.bbc.co.uk/go/pr/fr/-/2/hi/americas/4225013.stm.

censor these publications, school officials must show that the material is either unlawful or substantially disruptive to the school.

Resisting the *Hazelwood* Restrictions

Hazelwood gives public school systems more leeway in censoring nonpublic forum student writing thought to be offensive, mischievous, subversive, or insubordinate. Nevertheless, some states, school districts, and individual schools have chosen to overwrite *Hazelwood* by creating policies based on the older *Tinker* standard that gives students more freedom of expression. For example, shortly after the *Hazelwood* ruling, Massachusetts passed a law strengthening the First Amendment rights of students. It declared that "the right of students to freedom of expression in the public schools of the commonwealth shall not be abridged, provided that such right shall not cause any disruption or disorder within the school."[26]

Students in California have been able to rely on the California Student Free Expression Law that grants them added protection against administrative censorship of the student press. The law grants students freedom of speech and the press in all forums except when their expression is found to be obscene, libelous, slanderous, disruptive, or dangerous. Similarly, advocates of student free speech who objected to the *Draudt* decision passed the 2004 Colorado Newspaper Theft Law. Recognizing that confiscation of free-distribution newspapers by those who object to the newspapers' content is a frequent problem for the student press, the state law explicitly makes the seizure of free newspapers a crime in Colorado.

In contrast to these measures, many other states and schools have used the *Hazelwood* standard to intensify control over and even censor the student press. In reaction to the added restraint, so-called underground or unofficial student publications have gained popularity once again, much like they did during the 1960s. Due to rapid developments in computer technology and the World Wide Web, many underground publications are now Internet-based 'zines or blogs rather than print newspapers.

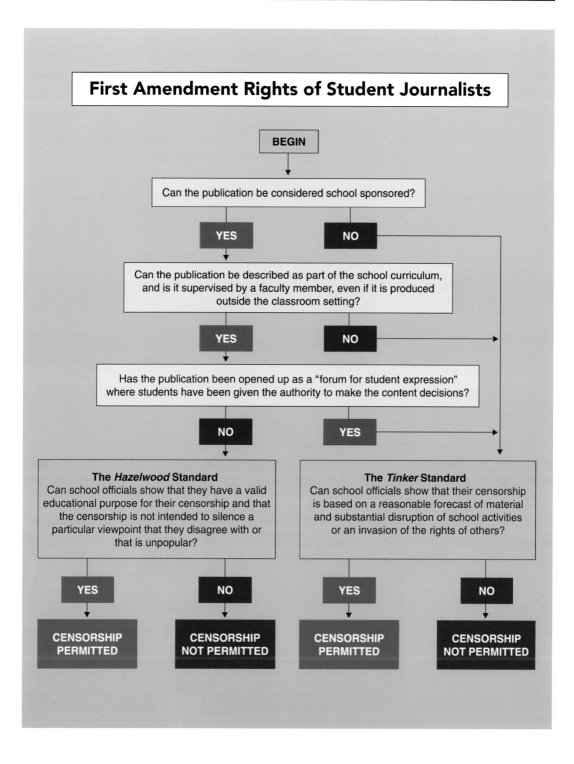

First Amendment Rights of Student Journalists

BEGIN

Can the publication be considered school sponsored?

YES — NO

Can the publication be described as part of the school curriculum, and is it supervised by a faculty member, even if it is produced outside the classroom setting?

YES — NO

Has the publication been opened up as a "forum for student expression" where students have been given the authority to make the content decisions?

NO — YES

The *Hazelwood* Standard
Can school officials show that they have a valid educational purpose for their censorship and that the censorship is not intended to silence a particular viewpoint that they disagree with or that is unpopular?

YES — NO

The *Tinker* Standard
Can school officials show that their censorship is based on a reasonable forecast of material and substantial disruption of school activities or an invasion of the rights of others?

YES — NO

CENSORSHIP PERMITTED

CENSORSHIP NOT PERMITTED

CENSORSHIP PERMITTED

CENSORSHIP NOT PERMITTED

More Freedom for Student Internet Publications

One of the first cases to consider whether the liberal *Tinker* standard or the more conservative *Hazelwood* standard should govern student speech on Internet Web sites was the 1998 *Beussink v. Woodland R-IV School District* case. Brandon Beussink was a junior at Woodland High School in Marble Hill, Missouri. He developed a homepage on the Web that expressed criticism of the school's principal and a teacher using what the court described as "crude and vulgar" language.[27] When the homepage came to the attention of principal Yancy Poorman, he demanded that Beussink remove the page, which he did. Nevertheless, Poorman suspended the student for ten days. The lengthy suspension resulted in Beussink's flunking all of his junior-year classes because of the school's absenteeism policy.

Beussink took the school district to court and won an injunction against the discipline on First Amendment grounds. Presiding district judge Rodney Sippel found that Beussink's homepage was not subject to *Hazelwood* standards because the publication was created off campus. Furthermore, using the *Tinker* standard,

Ryan Dwyer and his parents announce their lawsuit against their school district after it sanctioned the boy for content on his personal Web homepage.

the court found that the homepage had not caused disruption at the school and therefore was protected. Sippel wrote, "Disliking or being upset by the content of a student's speech is not an acceptable justification for limiting student speech under *Tinker*."[28]

Freedom of the Press and College Newspapers

The Supreme Court's *Hazelwood* decision dealt only with high school student publications. While a few college and university officials have tried to extend the *Hazelwood* standard to apply to their campuses, courts have consistently ruled against the power of administrators to censor school-sponsored student expression in higher education. That does not mean that college newspapers are free from censorship struggles. A case in point happened at Governors State University in Atlanta, Georgia.

In October of 2000 the Governors State dean of student affairs, Patricia Carter, ordered Regional Publishing, the newspaper's printer, to cease production of the school newspaper, the *Innovator*. Carter objected to a series of articles that were critical of the university administration. Jeni Porche, the *Innovator*'s editor in chief, and two other *Innovator* staff members sued, stating that their First Amendment rights were violated.

DO YOU THINK HIS WORDS DESERVE PUNISHMENT?

A University of New Hampshire student was banned from his English class after publishing in a blog violent and sexual content about other students and his teacher. He threatened to kill his girlfriend and stated, "[I] thought it would be cool to take a sawed-off shotgun to the undead faces of every freshman in my dorm."

National Student, "Student Banned for Violent Blog," July 5, 2005. www.nationalstudent.co.uk/International%20news/Story%20Student%20banned%20for%20violent%20blog.htm.

The case moved through the court system until the U.S. Court of Appeals for the Seventh Circuit finally ruled unanimously in favor of the students. The three-judge panel said that the constitutional rights of college student journalists cannot be limited by the *Hazelwood* standard:

> According to U.S. Census Bureau statistics . . . only 1 percent of those enrolled in American colleges or universities are under the age of 18, and 55 percent are 22 years of age or older. . . . Treating these students like 15-year-old high school students and restricting their First Amendment rights by an unwise extension of *Hazelwood* would be an extreme step for us to take absent more direction from the Supreme Court.[29]

Although decisions like this one favor free speech rights for college journalists, college administrators still try to exercise some control over the content of their schools' publications. Sometimes indirect methods are more successful than outright censorship. For example, a college is within its rights to fire the newspaper adviser in charge of directing student editors and reporters. In recent years, the tendency to dismiss the adviser when administrators disagree with a newspaper's content has become so common that the professional organization College Media Advisers (CMA) labeled 2004 "The Year of Advising Dangerously."

While administrators argue that firing journalism advisers allows them to protect the university from lawsuits and encourages responsible student journalism, others view the practice as an unethical form of censorship. When an adviser at Kansas State University was dismissed in 2004 after a minority student group criticized his coverage of diversity issues, the Society of Professional Journalists (SPJ) called Kansas State's action a "clear violation of the principles of free speech and a free press."[30]

Whether direct or indirect, censorship is a hot-button issue that continues to generate strong feelings in Americans. The issue of how much press freedom should be permitted in a democracy is further complicated when the reporters and editors are students and their work appears in an educational context. Americans cherish freedom of speech, but they also strive to protect individual privacy and educational integrity. Decisions about the freedom of student media publications are tricky when these competing interests collide.

RELIGIOUS LIBERTIES IN THE SCHOOLS

For many Americans, the United States is defined by its democratic government. To them, the free and diverse nation envisioned by the founders in the Declaration of Independence is the essence of America, a country in which all individuals can seek "life, liberty, and the pursuit of happiness" as long as they follow fundamental laws to ensure that the rights of others are not compromised.[31] According to this view, the separation of religion and the state mandated in the Bill of Rights ensures that the democratic government remains independent from religious influence.

Other Americans, however, argue that the United States is defined by fundamental Christian values cherished by some of the founders and incorporated in the country's founding document. In their viewpoint, Christian values are inseparable from other democratic principles and contribute to the education of U.S. students in and out of the classroom. They claim that the authors of the U.S. Constitution never intended to separate church and state and cite founders such as John Jay, the first chief justice of the United States, who said, "It is the duty of all wise, free and virtuous governments to countenance and encourage virtue and religion."[32] When it comes to public education, proponents of both sides of this issue have battled throughout history for the authority to determine how children are taught in the United States.

Establishment vs. Free Exercise

The principal legal precedent regulating the relationship between the church and the state comes from a section of the First Amendment to the U.S. Constitution, that states, "Congress

Opponents of school prayer show their support for a federal court decision to end organized prayer and bible study in Mississippi schools.

shall make no law respecting an establishment of religion, or prohibiting the free exercise thereof."[33] The first element of this statement is known as the establishment clause and ensures religious freedom for all by protecting against the governmental endorsement of any one religious view. In the 1947 Supreme Court case *Everson v. Board of Education*, the Court defined the establishment clause in this way:

> Neither a state nor the Federal Government can set up a church. Neither can pass laws which aid one religion, aid all religions, or prefer one religion over another. Neither can force or influence a person to go to or remain away from church against his will or force him to pro-

fess a belief or disbelief in any religion. . . . No tax in any amount, large or small, can be levied to support any religious activities or institutions whatever they may be called, or whatever form they may adopt to teach or practice religion. Neither a state nor the Federal Government can, openly or secretly, participate in the affairs of any religious organizations or groups and vice versa.[34]

In essence, the Court stated that the establishment clause puts a wall of separation between church and state.

To deal with the establishment issue, the Supreme Court devised a three-part test to determine the proper boundary between church and state. The test asks whether or not a government action fulfills a clear secular purpose, whether or not it advances or inhibits religion as its primary effect, and whether or not it avoids excess entanglement with religion. These three conditions are usually at the heart of the Supreme Court's judgment in cases related to the association of government with religion, and public schools have been an important context for hashing out decisions about the degree of separation necessary between church and state.

LESS RELIGION IN SCHOOLS

School sponsorship of a religious message is impermissible because it sends the ancillary message to members of the audience who are nonadherents that they are outsiders, not full members of the political community, and an accompanying message to adherents that they are insiders, favored members of the political community.

Santa Fe Independent School Dist. v. Doe (99-62) 530 U.S. 290 (2000).

The second element of the First Amendment section on religion, known as the free exercise clause, protects individuals from the government hindering their religious expression. The clause, first and foremost, gives students the right to believe whatever religious doctrine they desire. Furthermore, the government, including the government's public schools, cannot force students' belief, punish their expression of religious belief, or lend its power to any side in a religious controversy.

Americans have disagreed about the boundaries that prevent establishment on one hand, and yet allow free exercise on the other, giving rise to struggles over educational issues such as school prayer, student religious activities, public funding for religious schools, and the teaching of creationism along with evolutionary theory.

School Prayer

In societies across the globe, many formal community activities start with a ceremonial recognition of their importance. In religious settings, that ceremonial custom is often a moment of

Schoolchildren hold hands in observance of a National Day of Prayer. Some Americans believe overt religious expression like this should be forbidden in public schools.

prayer or meditation. For some people who are religious, beginning community activities with a prayer seems natural and uplifting, and, they would argue, starting the school day with a moment of prayer helps to reinforce student moral values. Representative Ernest Istook of Oklahoma addressed the issue of what kind of religious expression is appropriate in light of the diversity of religious belief in a June 4, 1998, session of Congress: "Prayer is not divisive. Prayer is unifying. What is divisive is for people to teach that we should not respect the prayer of another person or that we should not respect prayer in general. If you teach your children that, shame on you. But if we want people to be united, [we must] give them the chance to come together and express things positively."[35]

In contrast to those who advocate organized school prayer, other Americans believe in forbidding any overt religious expression in public places, including public schools. Proponents of a clear separation between church and state believe that when school officials lead or encourage prayer among students, they clearly violate the establishment clause. For example, Barry W. Lynn, executive director of Americans United for Separation of Church and State, believes that mandatory school prayer does impose religion on students, and that

> there is no generic, nonsectarian prayer all faiths can agree on. Prayer between individuals and their God is deeply private and does not exist in a "one-size-fits-all" format. In any given community, there are diverse religious communities with different traditions and many people who have chosen no spiritual path at all. No prayer will please everyone. [Schools] must be neutral on religion to protect the rights of everyone.[36]

How, then, can public schools observe students' freedom of religion but also avoid official endorsement of religion? Largely by testing the constitutionality of religious practice in the courts. A landmark case that illustrates the competing principles in the two clauses (free exercise and establishment) is *Engel v. Vitale*, brought by the parents of ten students in New York in 1962. The students' school district required each student to recite this prayer at the beginning of each school day: "Almighty God, we acknowledge our dependence upon Thee, and we beg Thy blessings upon us, our parents, our teachers, and our Country."[37] The parents in *Engel* argued that the prayer was contrary to the beliefs of their children and that any religious expression in public school violated the establishment clause of the First Amendment. The school board countered that the prayer was nondenominational and could appeal to all religious views. Moreover, they said, students who did not want to recite the prayer were permitted to remain silent. To eliminate the prayer would be to take away other students' free exercise of religion.

The Supreme Court sided with the parents. Justice Hugo L. Black wrote the majority opinion for the Court, saying that "although these two clauses [establishment and free exercise] may in certain instances overlap," preventing the establishment of state-sponsored religion was more important in this case. He said that "a union of government and religion tends to destroy government and degrade religion."[38] The case set a clear precedent that declared organized school prayer to be unconstitutional. According to the precedent, schools must not give the impression that they endorse religious belief over nonbelief or any particular belief over others.

Voluntary Student Religious Activities

While prayer led by school officials is clearly banned by the Supreme Court, some students have argued that they should be able to participate in religious activities if they voluntarily seek to do so during extracurricular activities. In some instances, for example, students have asked to open an athletic event by reciting a prayer. Others have volunteered to read a prayer during their graduation ceremonies. They argue that since the prayer is voluntarily offered outside of the classroom, they are not imposing religion on others.

Opponents have objected to prayer in these settings as well as in more formal educational situations. The problem cited in such cases is that student-led prayer constitutes peer pressure around religious practices. Legal suits contesting prayer during extracurricular activities have reached the Supreme Court,

Graduating seniors recite the Lord's Prayer in defiance of a Kentucky court ruling against prayer in school.

where decisions have consistently ruled that prayer is unconstitutional. For example, in the 2000 case of *Santa Fe Independent School District v. Doe*, the Court ruled that a pregame prayer given by a student at high school football games *does* violate the establishment clause. However, in line with the free exercise clause of the First Amendment, students have been allowed to engage in voluntary *individual* prayer, as long as it does not disrupt the educational mission of the school.

Other controversial forms of student religious practices include off-campus activities during school time and religious clubs. The legality of off-campus events came into question in 1952 when students in New York were released during the school day to participate in activities at religious centers away from school grounds. Students whose families chose not to participate in the release program stayed at school. When some objected to the religious activity during school hours, the Supreme Court heard the case. By a 6–3 vote, the Court held that noncoercive off-campus release time programs are permissible accommodations of the religious needs of students, and do not violate the establishment clause of the Constitution.

MORE RELIGION IN SCHOOLS

A Congress that allows God to be banned from our schools while our schools can teach about cults, Hitler and even devil worship is wrong, out of touch, and needs some common sense.

Rep. James Traficant, quoted in Hannah Proferl, "The Right Gets It Wrong About Religion," *Aquin*, April 22, 2005. www.stthomas.edu/aquin/042205/00042205.pdf, p. 9.

Much like off-campus religious activities, religious clubs in public secondary schools have traditionally been allowed as long as they are noncurriculum-related groups. The Equal Access Act (EAA), passed by Congress in 1984 and upheld as constitutional by the Supreme Court in 1990, makes it "unlawful for any public secondary school that receives federal funds and which has a limited open forum to deny equal access or a fair opportunity to, or discriminate against, any students who wish to conduct a meeting within that limited open forum on the basis of religious, political, philosophical, or other content of the speech at such meetings." A "limited open forum" is created whenever a public secondary school provides an opportunity for one or more "noncurriculum-related groups" to meet on school premises during noninstructional time. The forum is said to be limited because only the school's students can take advantage of it. However, the EAA states that "employees or agents of the school or government" must not participate with students in religious activities. If they are present, they must only monitor the activity "in a nonparticipatory capacity."[39]

Can Dress Codes Ban Religious Clothing?

Another controversy over religious freedom concerns students wearing religious symbols and clothing in school. Legal decisions in the United States have generally supported the right of schools to adopt dress codes to regulate student appearance; however, the courts have not allowed schools to ban any particular religious attire. A case in point involved a sixth-grade Muskogee, Oklahoma, student who wore a *hijab*, a traditional headscarf, to school in 2003 in order to practice the requirements of the Muslim religion to which she had recently converted. Like many other school districts across the nation, Muskogee had a "no head covering" dress code in place because gangs in the area often wore colored bandanas on their heads to identify themselves. The purpose of the ban was to curb gang activity in school. When school officials asked her to remove her *hijab* and obey the dress code, eleven-year-old Nashala Hearn refused and was suspended.

With the help of the Rutherford Institute, a Virginia-based civil liberties organization, Hearn's family sued the school district in 2004 for compromising the girl's right to free speech and free exercise of religion. When the United States Justice Department joined the suit in support of Hearn, the school decided to settle the case out of court. Hearn was allowed to return to school and wear her *hijab* without being penalized. Commenting on the case, assistant U.S. attorney general for civil rights

Nashala Hearn (left) was suspended for breaking her school's dress code by refusing to remove her traditional headscarf.

R. Alexander Acosta stated that "this settlement reaffirms the principle that public schools cannot require students to check their faith at the schoolhouse door."[40]

In the same year that the Hearn family settled their lawsuit, the nation of France passed a law to prohibit the wearing of conspicuous religious clothing in public schools as a matter of maintaining a strict separation of church and state. The law included a ban on the wearing of headscarves by Muslim girls in school. The U.S. Helsinki Commission, a federal agency made up of members of the House of Representatives and the U.S. Departments of State, Defense, and Commerce, filed a statement in reaction to the French law. The purpose of the Helsinki Commission is to monitor compliance with the Helsinki Accords of 1975, an international agreement among several countries, including the United States and France, to enforce certain human rights, including the rights to freedom of religion and freedom of speech. Helsinki Commission chairman Christopher H. Smith firmly denounced the law: "I urge French authorities to rethink their policy and make reasonable accommodations for students to wear religious dress. Expelling children is not the answer. Students attending public schools should not have to sacrifice their religious beliefs to enjoy the same educational opportunities as their fellow classmates."[41]

According to the Helsinki Commission, the right to wear a Muslim *hijab* should not only be a right for U.S. students, it should be an international right.

Public Funding for Religious Schools

Another hot-button controversy in education today is the issue of school choice. School choice debates stem from the fact that several different school systems exist in the United States, yet only public schools are supported by tax dollars. Parents who prefer to send their children to private schools have argued that they are at an economic disadvantage. Since the private schools receive no state support, parents have to pay tuition to the schools in order for children to attend. Some parents contend that this additional economic burden is particularly unfair when they want their children to attend religious school. Since no religious education is available in free public schools, they believe they are in effect having to pay for their religious freedom, an unconstitutional burden.

Proponents of broader school choice argue that students should be able to attend religious schools whether or not they can afford private school tuition. Nobel Prize–winning economist Milton Friedman proposed a plan to give parents vouchers to defray the cost of tuition if they want to send their children to private and religious schools. In his plan, the government would

Do School Vouchers Threaten Our Democracy?

The following is a statement by the Anti-Defamation League (ADL), an organization that works to ensure justice and fair treatment for Jewish people and all citizens of the United States.

Most Americans believe that improving our system of education should be a top priority for government at the local, state and Federal levels. Legislators, school boards, education professionals, parent groups and community organizations are attempting to implement innovative ideas to rescue children from failing school systems, particularly in inner-city neighborhoods. Many such groups champion voucher programs. The standard program proposed in dozens of states across the country would distribute monetary vouchers (typically valued be-

tween $2,500– $5,000) to parents of school-age children, usually in troubled inner-city school districts. Parents could then use the vouchers towards the cost of tuition at private schools—including those dedicated to religious indoctrination.

Superficially, school vouchers might seem a relatively benign way to increase the options poor parents have for educating their children. In fact, vouchers pose a serious threat to values that are vital to the health of American democracy. These programs subvert the constitutional principle of separation of church and state and threaten to undermine our system of public education.

Anti-Defamation League, "School Vouchers: The Wrong Choice for Public Education," 2001. www.adl.org/vouchers /vouchers_main.asp.

pay most of the private school tuition in order to ensure that all students could choose the type of school they preferred. Defenders of voucher programs say that such government assistance does not violate the establishment clause because government assistance is already available for some secular services in religious schools. For example, Pennsylvania and New Jersey allocate funding for textbooks, testing, and other services for private school students. In June 1998 the Supreme Court of Wisconsin ruled in favor of the Milwaukee Parental Choice Program, which provides financial assistance to low-income children who want to attend private and religious schools.

Opponents of school voucher programs object to governmental assistance on several grounds. They assert that state funding has a primary effect of advancing religion if it is channeled to religious schools. Such an entanglement would violate the establishment clause by blurring the division between church and state. Moreover, if tax dollars are funneled to private schools, they fear that public schools will suffer from the budget cuts necessary to spread limited funding to more institutions. The U.S. Supreme Court has not yet ruled whether or not school voucher programs are constitutional under the establishment clause.

Teaching Evolution, Teaching Religion

Debates over the proper content of public school curricula have also produced controversy about whether or not public schools can teach a religious viewpoint. These debates most often pit science-based theories of the creation of the earth and the universe against religious beliefs. In 1925 one of the most famous court cases in American history marked the educational dilemma caused by the growing popularity of Charles Darwin's theory of evolution. By that time, evolution was achieving scientific authority over the previously preferred creationist theory based on biblical teachings. A biology teacher in a rural Tennessee town, John T. Scopes, challenged the law that prohibited him from teaching about evolution. Famed lawyer Clarence Darrow argued the teacher's case in *Tennessee v. Scopes*, and eventually won the case that came to be called the "Monkey Trial" because Darwin's theory linked humans to other primates. However, the decision came

The Anti-Evolution League holds a book sale during the historic 1925 case,
Tennessee v. Scopes, *in which the teaching of evolution was at issue.*

out of the state supreme court and therefore affected only the law
in Tennessee.

Forty years later, another teacher had to challenge a similar
law in Arkansas. In 1965 Susan Epperson, a tenth-grade biology teacher in Little Rock, Arkansas, argued that she should be
able to teach the theory of evolution. In a unanimous decision,
the Supreme Court held that a state's control over the public
school curriculum does not include the right to withdraw from
the curriculum secular material that is at odds with certain religious beliefs. The decision declared that any ban on teaching
the theory of evolution violates the establishment clause.

Struggles over teaching creationism versus evolution continue in spite of the decision. Advocates of teaching creationism passed laws in Arkansas and Louisiana requiring the teaching of "creation science" in all public school courses that taught evolutionary theory. In 1987 a group of parents, teachers, and religious leaders challenged the Louisiana statute, taking their case all the way to the U.S. Supreme Court. In a 7–2 decision, the Court held that the so-called Creationism Act of Louisiana was

Should Schools Teach Creationism *and* Evolution?

Two thousand adults responded to a 2005 survey about creationism and evolution conducted by the Pew Research Center:

Most Americans (64%) say they are open to the idea of teaching creationism along with evolution in the public schools, and a substantial minority (38%) favors replacing evolution with creationism in public school curricula. While much of this support comes from religious conservatives, these ideas, particularly the idea of teaching both perspectives, have a broader appeal. Even many who are politically liberal and who believe in evolution favor expanding the scope of public school education to include teaching creationism. But an analysis of the poll also reveals that there are considerable inconsistencies between people's beliefs and what they want taught in the schools, suggesting some confusion about the meaning of terms such as "creationism" and "evolution."

Despite the growing national debate over the teaching of evolution, there is little evidence that school discussions of evolution are upsetting to students. Just 6% of parents with children in school say their child has mentioned feeling uncomfortable when the subject of evolution comes up at school. Comparably small numbers of parents say their children have expressed unease when the subjects of religion or homosexuality have come up at their child's school.

Pew Research Center, "Religion a Strength and Weakness for Both Parties, Public Divided on Origins of Life," August 30, 2005. http://people-press.org/reports/display.php3?PageID=988.

Source: R.J. Matson, *The St. Louis Post-Dispatch*/Cagle Cartoons.

"ON THE BRIGHT SIDE, WHEN YOU FALL ASLEEP IN CREATION SCIENCE CLASS, THE TEACHER THINKS YOU'RE PRAYING!"

intended to promote religion and therefore violated the establishment clause.

It is important to remember that the Supreme Court has made clear that instruction *about* religion in public schools is constitutional. However, decisions have required that religion must be taught objectively and neutrally. According to precedent, the purpose of public schools is to educate students about a variety of religious traditions, not to promote one religion or indoctrinate students into any specific faith tradition.

CHAPTER 5

STUDENTS' RIGHT TO PRIVACY

The issue of student privacy changed forever after April 20, 1999. It was on that day that Dylan Klebold and Eric Harris exploded homemade bombs and opened fire on fellow students at Columbine High School in Littleton, Colorado. The two teens brought an arsenal of weapons, including semiautomatic shotguns, into the school in duffle bags and hidden in their coats. They killed twelve students and a teacher, injuring dozens more before turning their guns on themselves. The Columbine massacre was not the first incident of school violence in the United States, yet Columbine was unique not only for the extent of the violence but also because school surveillance cameras videotaped students scattering to hide under library and cafeteria tables as the gunmen picked off their victims. The images were broadcast globally, making it one of the most recognizable episodes of school violence in history. Columbine shocked the world and provoked unprecedented examination of school environments. Many people called for more attention to be paid to all the dangers possible in educational settings, especially those involving violence and drug use. Some questioned whether policies regulating students' right to privacy were too permissive, thus encouraging students to risk concealing weapons or stashing illegal substances at school.

The issue of privacy in the schools pits students' personal rights against the schools' obligation to keep students safe from harm—from each other, from outsiders, and from themselves. When does an individual's privacy compromise the safety or educational experience of another student or teacher? In recent years, this issue has been especially contentious in relation to the search and seizure of students and their property, and in regard to policies about testing students for drug use. Another ongoing discussion in the area of student privacy involves differing opinions about the maintenance and distribution of student records.

School Safety vs. Individual Privacy

In the United States, the legal parameters of a person's right to privacy are defined in the Fourth Amendment to the U.S. Constitution. The Fourth Amendment ensures "the right of the people to be secure in their persons, houses, papers, and effects, against unreasonable searches and seizures."[42] In the world outside of school, police officers and government agents cannot search a

Family members of victims review photos of the Columbine shootings. The Columbine massacre made many question whether students' privacy rights compromise school safety.

A student undergoes a metal dectector sweep, one of many security measures enacted to prevent high school students from bringing weapons on campus.

home or person without a search warrant issued by a judge and based on probable cause that a crime has been committed.

Yet in the context of public education, the proper role of law enforcement and search-and-seizure practices has always been contentious. Due to the recent attention on school violence and student drug use, many schools have installed metal detectors that can locate concealed weapons, such as knives and guns, at their entrances. In some school districts, all students are subject to body searches before entering school buildings. More and more schools have also started to perform random searches of student lockers and desks. Such measures are often a part of zero-tolerance policies that immediately suspend or expel students carrying weapons or drugs. What constitutes a weapon varies in different school policies, but most schools ban explosives, guns, and knives at the very least. Some students, parents, and teachers praise strict measures to ensure school safety. Others consider them overly harsh and express concern that the privacy rights of students are being compromised.

Student Searches

The courts have provided guidance to school officials on the issue of student searches. A landmark Supreme Court case, *New Jersey v. T.L.O.*, helped define the legal justifications for a student search and the legal scope of a student search. The case involved a fourteen-year-old student who was discovered smoking, in violation of school rules. When the student denied smoking, the principal seized and searched her purse. The search yielded not only a pack of cigarettes, but also rolling papers and other items associated with drug use, a large amount of cash, and notes implicating the student as dealing in drugs. When the school brought delinquency charges against the student, her lawyers moved to suppress the evidence found in her purse, claiming that the principal violated her Fourth Amendment rights. The Court ruled in favor of the search and found that (1) a search of a student at its inception requires reasonable ground for suspecting the search will turn up evidence that the student is violating the law or school rules, and (2) the scope of the search must be reasonable based upon the facts surrounding the search. While the Supreme Court held that students have a legitimate expectation of privacy, a more flexible standard of "reasonableness" for searches of students is necessary to ensure school safety and discipline.

The requirement of reasonable suspicion in *New Jersey v. T.L.O.* may seem to rule out broadly used devices and practices such as metal detectors, entrance searches, and random locker or desk searches. However, the courts also recognize the schools' right to set limits to students' expectations of privacy on school grounds or in school property. In general, the courts have allowed schools to conduct suspicionless searches when steps are taken to reduce the reasonable expectation of privacy. For example, a school may send home a letter explaining its policy of random unannounced locker searches at the beginning of each academic year. The notice would serve the function of legally informing students that they should consider lockers to be "public" and not "private" areas.

Mandatory Drug Testing

The court case of *New Jersey v. T.L.O.* may have clearly defined the legal limits of searching the *belongings* of students, but it did not resolve the question of when schools can search the *bodies* of students. Compulsory drug testing of students has become a very controversial issue related to students' right to privacy. Since the 1990s, a growing number of schools are requiring drug tests, first for students who participate in athletics and extracurricular activities, and more recently for all students enrolled. Drug abuse, especially the harmful effects of steroid use among young athletes who seek to increase their physical strength, has motivated many schools' testing policies. Moreover, President George W. Bush advocated drug testing in his 2004 State of the Union address, lending credibility to the practice in schools. Supporters of drug testing claim that it can help curb drug addiction by adults as well as youth. John Walters, director of the Office of National Drug Control Policy, believes that addiction to drugs often begins in adolescence. "If we can change that," he says, "we can change the face of substance abuse in the U.S. for generations to come. [Testing] is a powerful tool at a critical time in young people's lives."[43]

Is Random Drug Testing of Students Wrong?

A statement by Students for Sensible Drug Policy (SSDP):

> The federal government has recently ramped up its campaign to encourage schools to implement drug testing regimes and even offers grants to fund them. Meanwhile, representatives from drug testing companies are increasingly arranging presentations in front of local school boards to promote their products. As a result, some schools require students to submit to drug testing if they want to participate in any extracurricular activity.
>
> Unfortunately, student drug testing is ineffective, counterproductive, expensive and invasive. . . .
>
> The concerns about invasiveness and rights violations are self-evident.
>
> Forcing a student to urinate into a cup while a school official listens outside the stall undermines civics lessons on the Fourth Amendment. Moreover, schools should not be in the business of subjecting already body-conscious adolescents to this kind of humiliating experience.
>
> Just as alarming as the government's promotion of student drug testing is the emerging trend it has fueled regarding the erosion of students' rights and privacy in other areas. At many schools, students can expect unannounced searches of their persons, bookbags, and lockers—with or without cause.

Students for Sensible Drug Policy, "Students Rights and Privacy," 2006. www.ssdp.org/campaigns/srp.

In reaction to the growing trend of requiring drug tests in educational environments, individuals and organizations also are raising objections to imposed drug testing. Those against the practice often cite research that finds drug testing to be an ineffective method of discouraging drug use. They point to studies that conclude that the best way to reduce student drug abuse is to encourage their participation in extracurricular activities, and that the more students engage in extracurricular life, the less inclination they seem to have to experiment with drugs. Organizations such as the Rutherford Institute, the

American Academy of Pediatrics, and American Civil Liberties Union argue that requiring drug tests for athletics and clubs deters students from extracurricular activities—an effect that would likely increase drug use rather than decrease it. Furthermore, opponents find drug testing to be overly invasive and often inaccurate. Being subjected to a mandatory test can undercut any sense of trust a student has in teachers and administrators. Moreover, a certain small percentage of drug tests, including urinalysis, yield false positive results, and human error can add to inaccuracies. Opponents argue that a student's record could be permanently stained even if a bad test result is ultimately cleared. First and foremost, though, opponents argue that drug tests undermine students' right to privacy.

EXPERIENCING A RANDOM DRUG TEST

I felt they were accusing us and convicting us before they had given us a chance. It was horrible. Someone would stand outside the bathroom stall and listen.

Newshour Extra, Lindsay Earls, quoted in "Can Your School Test You for Drugs?" February 19, 2002. www.pbs.org/newshour/extra/features/july-dec01/sc_cases.html.

In spite of such objections, the courts have tended to rule in favor of schools that have implemented random drug testing. In the 1995 case *Veronia v. Acton*, the U.S. Supreme Court upheld suspicionless drug testing of school athletes. According to the decision, school athletes have lower expectations of privacy because they already face mandatory physical examinations. The Court also said that testing was justified because athletes engage in dangerous activity in sports. Under the influence of drugs, they would be more likely to injure themselves, and the necessary safety of student athletes supersedes the preservation of their right to privacy. Similarly, in the 2002 case *Board of Education v. Earls*, the Court upheld random testing of students who participate in nonathletic extracurricular activities, arguing that the tests were a reasonable means of preventing and detecting drug use. However, when a school in Lockney, Texas, became

Lindsey Earls (right) challenged her school district's drug testing policy. At left, a woman who lost her daughter to drugs displays a sign supporting the policy.

the first institution to require drug testing of all students in grades six through twelve, a federal court struck down the policy as unconstitutional.

Control over Student Records

Another issue of student privacy rights relates to the way schools keep records of academic and personal progress from kindergarten through college graduation. Schools typically record extensive, and sometimes intimate, information about students and their families for educational purposes. Collecting and storing this information has the potential to intrude on student privacy. Yet such information also potentially could enhance the ability of teachers, counselors, and other professionals to provide the best instruction and guidance for students. The question is how to maintain a reasonable balance between the individual's right to privacy and the school's need to know information related to its educational mission.

This issue came to a head during the turbulent decades after the mid-twentieth century. In the late 1960s and 1970s a rising number of people—especially young people—insisted on their First Amendment right to freedom of speech and engaged in protest against societal discrimination and government policies. Demonstrating their support of civil rights, women's liberation, and the anti–Vietnam War movement, they came under the suspicion of law enforcement. Americans gained a new awareness about the extent to which various government institutions keep written files on the lives and activities of individual citizens. This growing awareness of government record keeping made some people question whether their constitutional right to privacy was being compromised.

Concerned about government record keeping, parents and students sought to have more control over educational information and its distribution. They lobbied for the right to inspect their own educational files in order to know what information was being recorded. They also wanted to prevent schools from giving out personal information unless it was authorized and necessary to a student's educational progress. Their efforts developed into the Family Education Rights and Privacy Act (FERPA), also known as the Buckley Amendment. FERPA took effect on November 19, 1974.

FERPA

FERPA clearly defines students' right to privacy in school records, files, documents, and other materials. It applies to elementary, secondary, and postsecondary educational agencies that receive federal support, and therefore encompasses all public schools and any private schools that accept federal funding (as many do). The U.S. Department of Health and Human Services enforces the act and handles any complaints that arise. FERPA addresses academic records and health information maintained by schools.

Under FERPA, parents and legally independent students have control over the distribution of all information except basic "directory" information, such as a student's name, address, phone number, and date of birth. Parents and eligible students have the right to inspect and review educational records. If they dispute the information in the files, they can request that the school correct the record or allow them to place a statement with the record explaining their objections. Furthermore, schools must obtain written permission from the parent or eligible student to release information from a student's record. A few exceptions to this rule include releasing information to school officials with a legitimate educational interest, and to outside officials in cases of health and safety emergencies. Finally, schools must notify parents and eligible students of their rights under FERPA annually.

Students Grading the Work of Classmates

Sometimes unexpected issues related to student privacy rights emerge now that FERPA is the law. One such issue has come about because of new trends in student-centered instructional methods. The theory behind student-centered learning is that students will learn more and more, effectively, if they work together and teach each other in addition to learning directly from the teacher. In line with this reasoning, some teachers have students critique and possibly grade each other's work as a student-centered learning activity. Kristja Falvo, a mother of three students in Oklahoma schools, objected to this practice; she told the teachers that the practice embarrassed her children, one of whom threatened to quit school because other students teased him about his test scores. When the teachers and the school refused to stop the peer-grading activities, Falvo sued the school district.

Testifying in defense of the policy, LeRoy Rooker of the U.S. Department of Education argued that peer grading does not violate FERPA because the grades do not become official educational records until after they are recorded in the teacher's gradebook. Teachers also testified that peer grading is a valuable class activity because students do learn from grading one another's work. However, the U.S. Court of Appeals for the Tenth Circuit in Denver sided with the plaintiffs and declared that peer grading is illegal. This court concluded that "grades which students record on one another's homework and test papers

Should Students Know the Grades of Their Peers?

Linda Starr, a former teacher and the curriculum and technology editor for *Education World*, disagrees with the decision in the 2002 case *Owasso Independent School Dist. No. I-001 v. Falvo*. What do you think?

> Kristja Falvo, the Oklahoma mother who initiated the case, claimed that teacher grade books were educational records and that peer grading of class work or homework assignments violated the privacy of those records. Falvo was responding to a practice in which students in her children's school district exchange papers for grading and then read the grades aloud so the teacher can record them in a grade book. According to Falvo, one of her children— who suffers from a mild learning disability—was ridiculed and called a "dummy" by classmates when his grades were known and announced publicly. She objected both to the peer grading and to the practice of reading the grades aloud.
>
> In rendering their decision, the nine U.S. Supreme Court Justices unanimously agreed that peer grading does not violate a student's right to privacy.
>
> The practice of publicly announcing all students' grades, whether assignments have been self-graded, peer graded, or teacher graded, is despicable—potentially humiliating and divisive—and should be banned in all our Nation's schools.

Linda Starr, "Peer Grading vs. Privacy: The Supreme Court Rules," *Education World*, February 26, 2002. www.education-world.com/a_issues/issues279.shtml.

and then report to the teacher constitute 'education records' under FERPA."[44]

The controversy continued, however, and the case was appealed to the Supreme Court, which reversed the lower court's decision in 2002. The Court ultimately ruled that student graders were not acting for educational institutions—students only briefly handled material assigned by another, official representative—and are not covered, therefore, by FERPA. Peer grading remains an acceptable practice.

FERPA thus does not absolutely protect the privacy of students in all educational situations. Two other issues that do not fall under FERPA are in-school commercial activities and military recruiting.

Companies in Classrooms

Especially in years when public funding for education is trimmed by budget cuts, schools sometimes rely on private companies to donate money or educational materials to their programs. Businesses can be active proponents of improving education. However, corporate support of public education can come with a price. In some cases, classrooms are turned into centers for consumer research, where sensitive, private information on students and their families is collected under the guise of education.

Teachers hang a sign for a company that donated money to the school. Cash-strapped schools are increasingly turning to private businesses for donations.

There are many ways that companies can gather valuable information from students while building their market research into class activities. For example, New Jersey elementary school students were told to fill out twenty-seven-page booklet called *My All About Me Journal* as part of a cable television marketing survey. In another case, a technology firm donated free classroom computers and Internet access. What the children did not know is that the company monitored students' Web activity by age, gender, and zip code. Students in a Massachusetts school were asked to do a cereal taste test and then answer an opinion poll.

COMMERCIALISM IN CLASSROOMS

"Do children—our patients—go to school under contract to watch commercials? Unfortunately, for many the answer is yes. More than 8 million children watch computers or television in schools with demanding and persistent commercials."

Carden Johnston, "Commercialism in Classrooms," *Pediatrics* 107, no. 4 (2001). http://pediatrics.aappublications.org/cgi/content/full/107/4/e44.

When parents found out that their children were subjected to market research in school, they organized opposition to the practices. After hearing the complaints of angry constituents, two U.S. senators introduced legislation to address the problem in 2001. Senators Chris Dodd of Connecticut and Richard Shelby of Alabama called for an end to unauthorized access to student information by companies. Dodd explained the reasoning behind the legislation: "More and more, schools are being perceived not just as centers for learning, but centers for consumer research. Our children should be instilled with knowledge, not tapped for information on their spending habits. Their privacy, and that of their parents, should be respected, not exploited."[45]

The Dodd-Shelby Student Privacy Protection Act passed in Congress and requires school districts to develop policies, in consultation with parents, concerning the collection of personal information from students to be used for marketing. School districts will be required to notify parents of these policies and to offer parents the opportunity to opt their children out of participating in market research. The senators say that the reform bill will help ensure that schools remain centers of learning, not centers of commercial activity.

Military Recruiting

Another conflict over student information and records has prompted a new version of the Student Privacy Protection Act to be introduced in 2005. This time, the issue involves military recruiters in schools. As a result of a provision in the 2001 No Child Left Behind Act, military recruiters have access to students' personal information and educational records. When they visit a high school, recruiters can use information in student records to help them persuade students to join the army, navy, air force, or marines. The only way recruiters can be prevented from access is if the parents or students formally declare that they opt out of being contacted by the military. If schools refuse to give military recruiters information, they can lose all of their federal education funds.

An alternative approach to military recruiting has been proposed by parents and Representative Mike Honda of California. Rather than require opting out, those in opposition to the requirement say that the military should not have access unless parents and students formally opt in. In other words, military recruiters would not be able to view student files unless the student or parent has written a letter giving permission. Honda's Student Privacy Protection Act of 2005 is still going through the legislative process. It remains to be seen whether it will pass along with the earlier Act of 2001.

Ensuring the privacy rights of students is challenging in our modern information-hungry society. On the one hand, those who want to investigate students' property, bodies, and records argue compelling cases for more access to student information. On the other hand, students and their parents want to ensure that the basic civil liberties of young people are respected and enforced. With the constant development of new information-gathering technology, striking a balance between free access and privacy will become ever more complex in the future.

Chapter 1: The Right to Education Without Discrimination

1. Quoted in Kenneth Jost, "School Desegregation," *CQ Researcher Online* 14, no. 15 (April 23, 2004). http://library.cq press.com/cqresearcher/cqresrre2004042300.

2. *Brown v. Board of Education of Topeka*, 349 U.S. 483 (1954).

3. 102 Cong. Rec. 4515–16 (1956). www.cviog.uga.edu/ Projects/gainfo/manifesto.htm.

4. *Green v. County School Board*, 391 U.S. 430 (1968).

5. Federation for American Immigration Reform, "Anchor Babies: The Children of Illegal Aliens," June 2004. www.fairus. org/site/PageServer?pagename=iic_immigrationissuecen ters4608.

6. California Proposition 187 (1994). http://en.wikisource.org/ wiki/California_Proposition_187_(1994).

7. Quoted in David Masci, "Hispanic Americans' New Clout," *CQ Researcher Online* 8, no. 35 (September 18, 1998). http://library.cqpress.com/cqresearcher/cqresrre1998091800.

8. Quoted in Masci, "Hispanic Americans' New Clout."

9. Fourteenth Amendment, U.S. Constitution. www.usconsti tution.net/xconst_Am14.html.

10. Quoted in National Coalition for Women and Girls in Education, "Math and Science Get C+ on Report Card on Gender Equity," *IDRA Newsletter*, March 2000. www.idra.org/ Newslttr /2000/Mar/Reprint.htm.

11. Quoted in Richard L. Worsnop, "Gender Equity in Sports," *CQ Researcher Online* 7, no. 15 (April 18, 1997). http:// library.cqpress.com/cqresearcher/cqresrre1997041800.

Chapter 2: Students' Freedom of Speech

12. Quoted in David Greenberg, "The Pledge of Allegiance: Why We're not One Nation 'Under God,'" *Slate*, June 28, 2002. http://slate.msn.com/id/2067499.

13. David L. Hudson Jr., "Pledge of Allegiance in Public Schools," First Amendment Center, November 2005. www.first amendmentcenter.org/speech/studentexpression/topic.aspx? topic=pledge.

14. *Karr v. Schmidt*, 460 F.2d 609 (5th Cir. 1972).

15. Quoted in Shannon Larratt, "Should Freedom of Expression Be a Right?" *BMEZine.com*, November 21, 2002. www.bmezine.com/news/pubring/20021121.html.

16. Jennifer Boccia, "Tinker vs. Who?" *Oblivion*, Spring 2000. www.oblivion.net/oblivion/9/tinker_vs.php3.

17. *Bethel School District No. 403 v. Fraser*, 478 U.S. 675 2D (1986).

18. Mike Hiestand and Mark Goodman, "Internet Forces Courts to Wrestle With Private, Off-Campus Student Speech." *The First Amendment and the Media*, 2001. www.mediainstitute. org/ONLINE/FAM2001/Online_P.html.

Chapter 3: The Rights of the Student Press

19. Thomas Jefferson, letter to Col. Edward Carrington, January 16, 1787. http://odur.let.rug.nl/~usa/P/tj3/writings/brf/ jefl52.htm.

20. *New York Times Co. v. Sullivan*, 376 U.S. 254 (1964).

21. Nicholas D. Kristof, *Freedom of the High School Press*. Lanham, MD: University Press of America, 1983, p. 3.

22. Quoted in Diane Divoky, ed., *How Old Will You Be in 1984?* New York: Discuss, 1969, p. 2.

23. *Tinker v. Des Moines Independent Community School District*, 393 U.S. 503 (1969).

24. *Draudt v. Wooster City School District Board of Education*, 246 F.Supp. 2d 820, 825 (N.D. Ohio 2003).

25. First Amendment Schools, "What Is a Public Forum?" June 3,

2005. www.firstamendmentschools.org/freedoms/faq.aspx?id=13012&SearchString=What_is_a_public_forum.

26. *Mass. Ann. Laws*, ch. 71, d 82 (2001).

27. *Beussink v. Woodland R-IV School District*, 30 F.Supp.2d 1175 (E.D.Mo. 1998).

28. *Beussink v. Woodland School District.*

29. *Hosty v. Carter*, 325 F.3d 945, 948 (7th Cir. 2003).

30. "Shooting the Adviser," *Editor & Publisher*, April 2005, p. 25.

Chapter 4: Religious Liberties in the Schools

31. Declaration of Independence. http://www.archives.gov/national-archives-experience/charters/declaration.html.

32. John Jay, speech delivered on November 4, 1800, in *The Speeches of the Different Governors to the Legislature of the State of New York, Commencing with those of George Clinton and Continued Down to the Present Time.* Albany: J.B. Van Steenbergh, 1825, p. 66.

33. First Amendment, U.S. Constitution, www.usconstitution.net/xconst_Am1.html.

34. *Everson v. Board of Education*, 330 U.S. 1 (1947).

35. Quoted in Patrick Marshall, "Religion in Schools," *CQ Researcher Online* 11, no. 1 (January 12, 2001). http://0-library.cqpress.com.bianca.penlib.du.edu:80/cqresearcher/cqresrre2001011200.

36. Quoted in Marshall, "Religion in Schools."

37. Quoted in Jamin B. Raskin, *We the Students: Supreme Court Cases for and About Students.* Washington DC: CQ Press, 2003, p. 73.

38. *Engel v. Vitale*, 370 U.S. 421 (1962).

39. Equal Access Act, 20 U.S.C. 4071(a).

40. Associated Press, "Muslim Student, Oklahoma District Settle Hijab Lawsuit," First Amendment Center, May 20, 2004. www.firstamendmentcenter.org/news.aspx?id=13379.

41. International Information Programs, "Helsinki Commission Leaders Alarmed at French Students' Expulsion over Reli-

gious Attire," November 4, 2004. http://usinfo.state.gov/dhr/Archive/2004/Nov/05-862094.html.

Chapter 5: Students' Right to Privacy

42. Fourth Amendment, U.S. Constitution. www.usconstitution.net/xconst_Amt.html.

43. Quoted in Sara B. Miller, "Steps Toward More Drug Testing in Schools," *Christian Science Monitor*, May 20, 2005. www.csmonitor.com/2005/0520/p01s04-ussc.htm.

44. *Falvo v. Owasso Independent School District*, 233 F.3d 1203 (10th Cir. 2000).

45. Quoted in Office of Senator Chris Dodd, "Dodd Acts to Protect Student Privacy," May 9, 2000. http://dodd.senate.gov/press/Releases/00/0509.htm.

DISCUSSION QUESTIONS

Introduction: Special Privileges, Special Limitations

1. Who were the first Americans to develop a public education system for children?

2. According to the author, what four developments in American history contributed to the idea that students should have special rights?

3. How does the author describe the student-centered educational philosophy that became popular in the early twentieth century?

Chapter 1: The Right to Education Without Discrimination

1. What was the purpose of the "common school" movement that emerged after the American Revolution?

2. How is the "separate but equal" court decision in *Plessy v. Ferguson* (1896) different from the "desegregation" decision in *Brown v. Board of Education* (1954)?

3. How has the Fourteenth Amendment been used in court cases to argue against segregation based on sex in military academies?

Chapter 2: Students' Freedom of Speech

1. What debate about students' rights was sparked when the wording of the Pledge of Allegiance was changed in 1954?

2. On what grounds does writer Shannon Larratt argue that students should be able to wear tattoos and body piercings openly in school?

3. How does the author define campus speech codes?

Chapter 3: The Rights of the Student Press

1. How is the court case *Tinker v. Des Moines* (1969) relevant to the rights of student journalists?

2. Why did Hazelwood East High School principal Robert Reynolds feel justified in censoring several pages of the student newspaper the *Spectrum* in the 1983 case *Hazelwood v. Kuhlmeier*?

3. What is the difference between a "public" and a "nonpublic" forum?

Chapter 4: Religious Liberties in the Schools

1. How does the establishment clause protect religious freedom?

2. According to the author, what is the intent of Milton Friedman's proposed voucher program for parents who want to send their children to private or religious schools?

3. Should public schools teach creationism?

Chapter 5: Students' Right to Privacy

1. In *Veronia v. Acton* (1995) what reasoning did the Supreme Court use to justify random drug testing for school athletes?

2. What is FERPA?

3. According to the author, why have some parents objected to military recruiters accessing information about their high school–aged children?

ORGANIZATIONS TO CONTACT

American Civil Liberties Union (ACLU)

125 Broad St. 18th Floor

New York, NY 10004-2400

(212) 549-2500

www.aclu.org

The ACLU is a national organization that defends Americans' civil rights guaranteed in the U.S. Constitution. It works to establish equality before the law, regardless of race, color, sexual orientation, or national origin and adamantly opposes regulation of all forms of speech, including student journalism and campus hate speech. The ACLU has national projects focused on specific issues, including students' rights. It offers numerous reports, fact sheets, and policy statements on a wide variety of issues. Publications include the position papers "Student Rights: Dress Codes and Uniforms," "Your Right to Religious Freedom," and "Hate Speech on Campus."

American Library Association (ALA)

50 E. Huron St.

Chicago, IL 60611

(800) 545-2433

www.ala.org

The American Library Association is the nation's primary professional organization for librarians. It works to educate the public about the importance of intellectual freedom and free speech in libraries. Through its Office for Intellectual Freedom, the ALA monitors and opposes efforts to ban books in schools. Publications include the bimonthly *Newsletter on Intellectual Freedom*, articles, fact sheets, and policy statements, including "Freedom to Read Statement" and "Freedom to View Statement."

Education Law Association (ELA)

300 College Park #0528

Dayton, OH 45469

(937) 229-3589 • (937) 229-3845

www.educationlaw.org

The Education Law Association is a nonprofit organization that provides information about the rights of students, parents, school boards, and school employees. The ELA publishes numerous newsletters, books, and monographs, including *The Law of Student Expulsions and Suspensions* and *A Legal Guide to Religion and Public Education.*

Electronic Frontier Foundation (EFF)
454 Shotwell St.
San Francisco, CA 94110-1914
(415) 436-9333 • fax: (415) 436-9993
www.eff.org

The Electronic Frontier Foundation works to protect privacy and freedom of expression in the arena of computers and the Internet. Its missions include supporting individual civil liberties protected in the First Amendment. The EFF advocates for student access to computer information and the freedom of student speech online. The organization publishes an electronic bulletin, *Effector*, and the guidebook *Protecting Yourself Online: The Definitive Resource on Safety, Freedom, and Privacy in Cyberspace.*

First Amendment Schools (FAS)
First Amendment Center at Vanderbilt University
1207 18th Ave. S.
Nashville, TN 37212
(615) 727-1600 • fax: (615) 727-1319
www.firstamendmentschools.org

First Amendment Schools is a joint project sponsored by the Association for Supervision and Curriculum Development and the First Amendment Center to help schools affirm First Amendment principles through their activities and policies. The organization focuses on preserving five fundamental freedoms for students and teachers: freedom of religion, speech, press, assembly, and petition. FAS offers teaching guides and resources, including *The First Amendment in Schools* and "Teaching About Religion in Public Schools: Where Do We Go from Here?"

Foundation for Individual Rights in Education (FIRE)
601 Walnut Street, Suite 510
Philadelphia, PA 19106
(215) 717-FIRE (3473) • fax: (215) 717-3440

The mission of FIRE is to defend individual rights at America's colleges and universities. These rights include freedom of speech, legal equality, due process, religious liberty, and sanctity of conscience. Publications include *FIRE's Guide to Free Speech on Campus* and *FIRE's Guide to Religious Liberty on Campus.*

The Freechild Project

PO Box 6185
Olympia, WA 98507-6185
(360) 753-2686
www.freechild.org

The Freechild Project was created in April 2000 to encourage young people to seek active roles in their schools and communities. The organization promotes social change led by and with young people around the world, particularly those who have been historically denied the right to participate. *The Freechild Newsletter* is published twice a month.

The Freedom Forum

1101 Wilson Blvd.
Arlington, VA 22209
(703) 528-0800 • fax: (703) 284-3770
www.freedomforum.org

The Freedom Forum is dedicated to free press, free speech, and other First Amendment rights. It sponsors conferences, educational guides, publications, broadcasting, online services, and other programs. The organization operates the Newseum, an interactive museum about journalism and the press. Position papers about students' rights include "The Silencing of Student Voices: Preserving Free Speech in America's Schools" and "The Bible and Public Schools."

Student Press Law Center (SPLC)

1101 Wilson Blvd., Suite 1100
Arlington, VA 22209-2275
(703) 807-1904
www.splc.org

The Student Press Law Center is a nonprofit organization devoted to educating high school and college student journalists about their First Amendment rights. The SPLC provides free legal advice to support the student news media and to combat censorship in educational environments. Numerous resources are available at the SPLC Web site, including "Frequently Asked Questions About Student Press Law" and "Student Media Guide to Internet Law."

FOR MORE INFORMATION

Books

Donald Altschiller, *Hate Crimes: A Reference Handbook*. 2nd ed. Santa Barbara, CA: ABC-CLIO, 2005. Examines cases of crimes committed against individuals because of their race, religion, sexual orientation, or ethnic background.

Gerald W. Bracy, *Bail Me Out! Handling Difficult Data and Tough Questions About Public Schools*. Thousand Oaks, CA: Corwin, 2000. Extensive statistics about public schools and student achievement.

Garrett Epps, *To an Unknown God: Religious Freedom on Trial*. New York: St. Martin's, 2001. Accounts of struggles for religious freedom and the battle that gave birth to the Religious Freedom Restoration Act of 1993.

Mike Godwin, *Cyber Rights: Defending Free Speech in the Digital Age*. rev. ed. Cambridge, MA: MIT Press, 2003. A compelling account of the most explosive and controversial issues surrounding freedom in cyberspace.

Kathleen Krull, *A Kid's Guide to America's Bill of Rights: Curfews, Censorship, and the 100 Pound Giant*. New York: Avon, 1999. Examination of the ten amendments to the U.S. Constitution that make up the Bill of Rights, explaining what the amendments mean, how they have been applied, and the rights they guarantee.

Douglas S. Reed, *On Equal Terms: The Constitutional Politics of Educational Opportunity*. Princeton, NJ: Princeton University Press, 2001. An analysis of educational reforms that improved educational access for different groups in society.

Harvey A. Silverglate and Josh Gewolb, *FIRE's Guide to Due Process and Fair Procedure on Campus*. Philadelphia: Foundation for Individual Rights in Education, 2003. Information for students about how academic misdeeds and behavioral misconduct are handled by colleges.

Periodicals

Mark Boal, "The Supreme Court vs. Teens," *Rolling Stone*, June 6, 2002.

Church & State, "Voters and Vouchers: The People Speak," January 2001.

David Glenn, "The War on Campus: Will Academic Freedom Survive?" *Nation*, December 3, 2001.

Charles Levendosky, "Voucher Decision Sidesteps Constitution," *Progressive Populist*, August 1–5, 2002.

David Masci, "Preventing Teen Drug Use: Is the 'Get Tough' Approach Effective?" *CQ Researcher*, March 15, 2002.

Welch Suggs, "Deadly Fuel: As Supplements and Steroids Tempt and Endanger More Athletes, What Are Colleges Doing?" *Chronicle of Higher Education*, March 14, 2003.

Ryoko Yamaguchi, Lloyd D. Johnson, and Patrick M. O'Malley, "Relationship Between Student Illicit Drug Use and School Drug-Testing Policies," *Journal of School Health*, April 2003.

Wendy Murray Zoba, "Church, State, and Columbine," *Christianity Today*, April 2, 2001.

Videos

Eyes on the Prize. Vol. 4. Episodes "Ain't Scared of Your Jails (1960–1961)" and "No Easy Walk (1961–1963)." Milton, MA: Blackside, 1995.

Eyes on the Prize. Vol. 7. Episodes "The Keys to the Kingdom (1974–1980)" and "Back to the Movement (1979–mid 1980s)" Milton, MA: Blackside, 1995.

Separate but Equal. VHS/DVD. Directed by George Steven Jr. Los Angeles: Republic Pictures Home Video, 1991.

Web Sites

Constitutional Topic: Student Rights, The U.S. Constitution Online (http://www.usconstitution.net/consttop_stud.html). A section of the U.S. Constitution Online directory, this site provides an overview of students' rights protected by the U.S. Constitution. It includes a summary of landmark court cases related to topics such as freedom of the press, freedom of expression, and search and seizure protections.

National Youth Rights Association (NYRA) (http://www.youthrights.org/). The Web site of the Maryland-based nonprofit organization, works to defend the civil and human rights of young people in the United States.

Youth Rights Information Archive (http://www.yria.alcade.net/). A comprehensive archive of news articles and essays about the rights of young people. Includes an extensive list of organizations that advocate on the behalf of youth rights.

INDEX

PICTURE CREDITS

ABOUT THE AUTHOR

Kate Burns lives in Denver, Colorado, with her partner, Sheila, and their cats and iguana. She received her Bachelor of Arts from Colorado State University and her Master of Arts from the University of California, San Diego. She currently works as a freelance writer and editor, and teaches writing at community colleges and universities near her home.